I'M HOSTING AS FAST AS I CAN!

I'M
HOSTING
as Fast as I Can!

Zen and the Art of Staying
Sane in Hollywood

TOM BERGERON

HarperOne
An Imprint of HarperCollins*Publishers*

HarperOne

I'M HOSTING AS FAST AS I CAN!: *Zen and the Art of Staying Sane in Hollywood.* Copyright 2009 by Tom Bergeron. All rights reserved. Printed in the United States of America. No part of this book may be used or reproduced in any manner whatsoever without written permission except in the case of brief quotations embodied in critical articles and reviews. For information address HarperCollins Publishers, 10 East 53rd Street, New York, NY 10022.

HarperCollins books may be purchased for educational, business, or sales promotional use. For information please write: Special Markets Department, HarperCollins Publishers, 10 East 53rd Street, New York, NY 10022.

HarperCollins Web site: http://www.harpercollins.com

HarperCollins®, 🏭®, and HarperOne™ are trademarks of HarperCollins Publishers

FIRST EDITION

Designed by Janet M. Evans

Library of Congress Cataloging-in-Publication Data
Bergeron, Tom.
    I'm hosting as fast as I can! : Zen and the art of staying sane in Hollywood / Tom Bergeron. — 1st ed.
       p. cm.
     ISBN 978-0-06-176587-2
   1. Bergeron, Tom. 2. Television personalities—United States—Biography. I. Title.
     PN1992.4.B47A3   2009
     791.4502'8092—dc22
     [B]

2008051447

09 10 11 12 13 RRD(H) 10 9 8 7 6 5 4 3 2 1

To Lois, Jessica, and Samantha,
my personal Three Pillars of Zen

CONTENTS

INTRODUCTION

THERE I STOOD, ON LIVE TELEVISION, WITH FORTY MILLION EYES ON me and an unconscious Osmond at my feet. Marie Osmond, moments after performing an energetic samba on *Dancing with the Stars,* had dropped like a sack of potatoes just to the left of my peripheral vision. I didn't see the faint, but I heard it. There was, as I recall, a slight whoosh followed by a resounding thud. Only after watching it on YouTube (where it was available almost before she hit the floor) did I see what our millions of viewers had seen.

For a second I thought she was kidding. Judge Len Goodman had been droning on about this or that (perceived) misstep in Marie's technique, and I thought she was using a comic swoon to suggest he wrap it up already. The audience at first let out an uncertain laugh. Then it fell silent. I turned, looked down, and saw her face. She was pale; her mouth hung open. (She *wasn't* kidding.) I knelt next to her, as did her professional dance partner, Jonathan Roberts. Then I did what anyone would do when faced with an emergency.

I threw to a commercial.

Suddenly, EMTs, producers, Marie's small entourage, and other *DWTS* staff joined us at her side. After a long twenty seconds, her eyes fluttered and her limbs came back to life. She blinked into focus, suddenly aware that she was on her back looking up at a circle of concerned faces. She glanced over at me, gave me a sick smile, and said, "Oh, crap!" I tried not to take it personally.

Truth is, "Oh, crap!" was pure poetry. It was funny, irreverent, and, given the circumstances, remarkably focused. Plus, now I had a punch line—a "Guess what she said when she came to?" opener to ease the audience's tension when we returned from our extended commercial break. Had she said, "I think I'm going to puke!" it wouldn't have been as helpful.

Marie was aided to her feet, and then, ever the performer, she offered a wobbly bow to the relieved and applauding studio audience. I couldn't help but smile, both in amazement and in admiration. Thirty seconds earlier she'd been out like a light, and now she was completely commanding the stage (albeit with slightly crossed eyes). When we returned to the air, she was sitting backstage, waiting to appear on camera to receive the judges' scores for her samba.

But first, the camera would be coming to me. I knew that the home audience, who hadn't seen Marie's comforting bow, was likely agonizing about her condition, and that it was *my* job as host to ease their concerns and get the show back on track. The viewers would initially see me in an overhead wide shot of the ballroom, so I made sure I was smiling and loose when the red light came on. *She can't be dead. Look, he's smiling!* the TV audience would think. As the shot changed to my close-up and the stage manager cued me, I knew that a casual tone would help, too. Ultimately, of course, the visual proof that Marie very much *wasn't* dead would seal the deal.

I explained that Marie had fainted and that she was fine. Then, savoring the moment, I shared her first words, which even the studio audience hadn't yet heard. At "Oh, crap!" the ballroom exploded with laughter, and I could only imagine a similar reaction in living rooms across America.

The backstage camera caught Marie's embarrassed grin. She shrugged. "Sometimes when I'm excited I forget to breathe," she said, at which point everyone else exhaled.

It's often said that comedy equals tragedy plus time. (*Other than that, Mrs. Lincoln, how did you enjoy the play?*) In this case, comedy equaled shock plus about seven minutes. And Neil Simon's Sunshine Boys were right. Words with *K* sounds *are* funnier.

Marie's comment that night brought to mind one of my favorite sayings, the essence of which I'd read years ago in a book by the late philosopher Alan Watts.

If you hold your breath, you lose it.

I always loved that. It's profound enough to launch a thesis and simple enough to fill a fortune cookie. And, despite Marie's ill-timed fainting and the ensuing commotion, *my* breathing had remained fairly steady, my focus reasonably clear. To be honest, I reacted less like a television host and more like a dad, as I would when my daughters were small and would skin a knee or fall off a swing. All my attention would turn to them. Same with Marie's sequined swoon. Getting us off the air so we could determine her condition barely required a thought. It was instinct. I couldn't imagine doing anything else.

Later, a number of people, including my friend and former *Dancing* contestant Jerry Springer (who knows a thing or two about handling commotion), complimented me on how calmly I responded. Live television, after all, doesn't give you any second takes.

And I *was* calm. I almost always *am* calm on live TV. Sometimes the hours I spend hosting *Dancing with the Stars* are the most relaxed hours of my day. That may sound odd given that most people surveyed actually fear public speaking more than their own death. Yes, they'd rather *cease to exist* than stand up in front of people and talk. Not me. Give me a live TV camera and twenty million viewers, and I'm as comfortable as a hedonist at a health spa. But that wasn't always true.

Not by a long shot.

CAN YOU HEAR ME NOW?

I T WAS A SATURDAY NIGHT IN 1972. I WAS A SEVENTEEN-YEAR-OLD high school senior, sitting alone in a dimly lit radio studio in my hometown of Haverhill, Massachusetts. I was barely aware of the music I'd put on the turntable. Other things competed for my attention, most prominently my nerves.

My heart hammered against my ribs. My throat tightened. I stared at the toggle switch, which controlled the microphone and the dial directly under it, which controlled its volume. I reached out to touch the switch . . . and then pulled back. *Oh, shit, what am I doing here? Why did I think I could do this?* I knew that the moment I flicked that switch and turned that dial, there'd be no turning back. My voice would be out there, "on the air," for the very first time.

Who would be listening? My family? Certainly. My friends? Sure. But who else? This was a 1,000-watt radio station. It was 6:10 on a Saturday night. Who knew how many others could be out there? Hell, there could be *dozens*! I tried to swallow but couldn't. My peripheral vision collapsed, and all I could see were the toggle switch and the dial, the toggle switch and the dial, the toggle switch and the dial . . .

The song was ending; the music was fading. Only seconds left. *Oh, shit, I have to pee. Or faint. Or both. First I'll faint and then I'll piss myself.* Gotta prioritize.

No, I had to do it. I *could* do it. I adjusted my headphones, flicked the switch to the right, and cupped my hand over the dial. The last notes of America's "A Horse with No Name" gave way to the crackle of the needle bouncing against the album's center. It was now or never. I turned the dial clockwise, took a deep breath, and, for the first time on the radio, said *my* name. I had officially begun my career as a broadcaster.

And I sucked.

Truly, I did. I'm not exaggerating. My proud grandfather recorded the entire six-hour show, and I eventually listened to about twenty minutes, just enough to consider entering the witness-protection program. I don't remember where those tapes disappeared to or what exactly I said in those first moments as a broadcaster. I do remember that my tone was akin to a dental patient trying to chat casually while watching the approaching Novocain shot; or like Barney Fife pretending to be James Bond. I wasn't fooling anyone—with the possible exception of my grandfather. He thought I did great. At least that's what he told me. Maybe he was just being supportive. A white lie or two for his only grandson. Of course, he'd lived through the Great Depression and World War II. He'd witnessed *real* disasters. Grading on that scale, I could've strangled kittens all night and still not been all that bad.

The Monday after my virgin broadcast, walking the corridors of Haverhill High between classes, I was quickly made aware of some other members of my radio audience.

"Hey, Bergeron," the ringleader of a small group of assho— . . . I mean, *students*—yelled, "heard you on the radio. You sucked."

See? It wasn't just *me* saying it.

But it wasn't all bad. It was mostly pretty damn good. Not my performance; you couldn't have saved that with an exorcism. I mean my situation. After all, I was a high school student actually being paid to host a radio show at a professional (well, more about that later) broadcast facility! Who cared if I sucked on my first attempt? Next Saturday night, I reasoned, when I flicked that switch and turned that dial, I'd suck a little less. And I'd be even less sucky the Saturday after that; assuming of course that the station manager was willing to keep paying a buck seventy-five an hour for only marginal leaps in quality.

Getting my foot and quavering voice in the door of the radio station, WHAV, was the culmination of a deliberate campaign hatched the moment I discovered that one of the high school's English teachers, Edwin Johnson, worked there part-time as a newscaster. I signed up for his public-speaking course and set out to impress the hell out of him. When, months later, he asked his brownnosing A student about his career goals, my answer exploded like a sneeze.

"Radio! I want to be on the radio!"

Upon hearing that, he generously offered to introduce me to WHAV's owner/station manager/sales manager/program director and hallway monitor, an eccentric and curmudgeonly chap named Ed Cetlin. I accepted the offer with similar sneezelike velocity. Within weeks, a meeting was scheduled. I was ecstatic. I was going to have a job interview at a radio station! My promising career as a supermarket-shelf stocker, begun in my freshman year, was about to be tossed aside like so much bad lettuce.

When I met Ed Cetlin, he asked me, "Why do you want to work in radio?" in a tone that suggested I'd aspired to developing carcinogens. He chewed on the ends of his glasses and squinted as he talked. I almost suggested he *wear* the glasses rather than gnaw on them, if only to help with the squinting, but thought better of it. Instead, I blathered on about my love for radio, how I'd always dreamed of being a broadcaster, and how hard I'd work if given the chance.

He shook his head in dismay. "You'll never make a living in radio. It's not a career. I'll prove it to you. I'll give you a job."

And, at a dollar seventy-five an hour, he set out to prove his point. But first, he said, I had to get my third-class operator's license. I'd need to learn how to take meter readings and monitor the transmitting equipment, a common requirement at low-power radio stations in the

1970s. To get that license, I'd take a test at the FCC office in the Customs House in Boston. No big deal. Until I took it, that is, and flunked.

If you hold your breath, you lose it.

I'd studied enough for the test, or so I thought. When my dad drove me to Boston on that overcast morning, I was convinced I would ace it. Passing it was a mere formality, hardly worth my time. I'd already given my notice at the supermarket and developed a bit of a confident swagger. No more mopping up smashed applesauce jars in aisle four for me, no sir. I was Tom Bergeron. I was gonna be on the radio!

Once inside the FCC office, I sat at a desk in a room much like my high school classrooms. Other aspiring broadcasters sat in rows at the other desks. I wondered if they had jobs waiting for them as I did. Probably not. Poor them. Then I began the test. Poor *me*.

My chest tightened. What was *this* question? I didn't study anything about this. And that one? How do you calculate that again? I looked around me. Everyone else seemed to be doing just fine—eyes on the prize and pencils on the page. I tried to focus, but the chatter in my head wouldn't stop. *Clean-up, aisle three! Clean-up, aisle four!* I could see applesauce jars dropping like hailstones.

Not long after I turned in the test, I was told I hadn't passed. Then I was told I had to wait three months to take it again. *Three months? Are you out of your mind? I've already given my notice!* I lost it. I began berating the FCC employee, downright questioning his competence and demanding he rescore the test. "I'll be happy to," he said, ignoring my tirade, "in three months."

My dad, who was both embarrassed and angered by my display, placed a firm hand on my back and moved me to the elevator. "Calm down," he said. "You're behaving like an idiot." He was being kind. My behavior that day was unbecoming to idiots. What's more, I was probably responsible for several FCC employees vowing never to have kids, especially seventeen-year-old kids.

In the throes of my tantrum, I was sure that it was all a conspiracy—that the job was lost and my life was over. I'm guessing my dad spent most of the ride home counting to ten and vowing to never have *more* kids. We stopped at a favorite Chinese restaurant on the way, and, much to my horror, sitting in a booth with his Moo Goo Gai Pan was Ed Cetlin. Could this day get any worse? I nervously approached him and said hello. I told him that I hadn't passed the test (I spared him my conspiracy theory) and that I wouldn't be able to take it again for three months. I braced myself for his reaction, which would no doubt trigger the whole "the job is lost and life is over" stuff.

"So take it again in three months," he said, barely looking up from his food. "We'll start you then."

"Huh?" I responded. I always was fast with the ad-libs.

"Look," he said, now squinting a bit in my direction, "you want to get into radio and ruin your life, you can do it just as easily in three months."

Crisis averted. But talk about a tantrum buzz kill.

Three months later, after dining on ample servings of humble pie, I returned to Boston with my dad, smiled ever so politely at the FCC guy, and once again took the test. This time, I passed. I had my third-class operator's license and my first job in radio. What I didn't yet have was a handle on my penchant for occasional temper tantrums.

Getting *that* was going to take a little longer.

2

THERE'S NO PLACE LIKE OM

QUITE OFTEN, IN THE HOUR BEFORE *DANCING WITH THE STARS* broadcasts live, a producer or two will come knocking on my dressing-room door with last-minute notes or news of the latest spray-tanned meltdown. Usually they find me just sitting in my favorite chair, from which I can reach to my right, open the door, and let them in. I'm not watching television, reading a book, peering into my laptop, or doing anything else that would be immediately apparent.

I'm just sitting.

I think they're used to it by now, but at first they'd stroll in, glance around for evidence of any other activity, and sit on the couch opposite me with nervous smiles. I understood why. People generally like to see other people doing *something*. It relaxes them. If you come across a person doing *nothing*, what's the first thing you think? Come on, be honest. You don't think, *Oh look, there's a person doing nothing.* You think, *I wonder what he's up to.*

When I was a teenager, I'd sometimes drive to my house and sit in the car for a few minutes listening to the radio while a song or a newscast finished. Almost without fail, I'd look up and see one or both parents peering anxiously at me from the front door. "What's the matter?" they'd ask. "Nothing," I'd answer, "just listening to something."

They'd nod, not quite convinced. "Oh, OK. We were worried because you were just sitting there."

In addition to the hours I spend in the gym each week, the time I spend *just sitting* or, more accurately, meditating are the among the most beneficial. My biceps, abs, and quadriceps aren't the only body parts I train. My mind gets its version of a bench press, too. I've meditated for years, sometimes regularly (for twenty minutes twice daily), sometimes sporadically (only a few times a week), and the mental workouts have paid off. Dude, my mind is *cut*.

OK, maybe I'm still sporting some synaptic love handles, but why quibble? The bottom line is that my meditation practice, which I originally began only to cool my hot temper, has greatly improved my overall mental and physical well-being.

What am I doing while I'm meditating? Am I really just sitting there doing nothing? Hardly. As with a gym workout, a meditation session requires effort, commitment, and focus. Especially focus. I happen to focus on the mental repetition of a Sanskrit mantra. You can just as easily focus on your breath, the flicker of a candle's flame, or a word that has a special meaning to you, such as *slower, calm, peace,* or *lasagna.*

You might be wondering why, given the wide range of things on which to meditate, I chose a supposedly mystical word from an ancient language. Easy. "Sanskrit mantra" sounds way cool, and I'm a meditation snob.

I'm kidding. I use that particular mantra because it came with the meditation training I paid for years ago. Now I'm not kidding. I paid for it, they gave it to me, and so I use it. That's how deep and mystical *I* am. I don't even remember what my mantra means, although I did Google it once. I just wanted to make sure it didn't mean "I'm Satan's bitch" or something like that. It doesn't. In my experience, it's not *what* you focus on as much as *that* you focus.

Sitting while you meditate, rather than lying down, is important. Lying down usually leads to falling sleeping, which tends to undermine the focusing a wee bit. Sit comfortably with your back supported. You don't have to twist yourself into a half or full lotus position. In fact, don't even try. Why chance cramping? It's hard to achieve inner peace while your muscles are seizing up.

Each time random thoughts intrude, and they will, simply return to the focal point. No judgment, no frustration; just acknowledge the thoughts, mentally sweep them away, and return. I often imagine the thoughts as Styrofoam pieces bobbing along a river current. When I become aware of them, I just imagine my arm gently moving them downstream. That may sound like one of those "easier said than done" steps, but it's really just that basic. Even after all my years of meditating, it often takes me a few minutes to get past the *Are we there yet? Are we there yet?* nagging chatter of my mind. Once I do, however, the sensation of calm and connectedness is profound.

Before strolling onto a set, whether for *Dancing with the Stars, America's Funniest Home Videos,* or a guest spot on a talk show, I meditate. Sometimes I'll sit alone for twenty minutes in my dressing room; sometimes I'll spend twenty seconds finding my center amid a crowded backstage. After close to thirty years of practice, finding that quiet place is usually easier than remembering where I left my car keys.

In the case of *Dancing with the Stars,* for example, ten minutes before our live broadcast the backstage area is swarming with celebrities, dancers, makeup and hair people, wardrobe people, managers, publicists, assistants to the stars, and assorted hangers-on. In smaller, huddled groups, minor adjustments are made to the minor amounts of fabric that constitute the women's costumes. Photos are taken, makeup is finalized, backslaps of good luck are exchanged. Some couples use any available square footage to, quite literally, squeeze in one last rehearsal. Meanwhile, onstage (or, in the show's lingo, "in the ballroom"), our warm-up guy is operating at full throttle, energizing the five hundred audience members and teaching them how to applaud and cheer on cue. The energy is exciting, chaotic, and sometimes deafening.

In the midst of it all, I meditate.

I weave my way through the backstage throng to a narrow area adjacent to the stage that serves as our on-deck circle. There, waiting to be introduced, I make sure I'm totally present, completely in the moment. No obsessing about anything that may have happened earlier, no worrying about anything that could happen later. Be here. Now.

That's the reason I love live television so much. By its very nature, it keeps me focused. It's not something that, if my attention wanders and I screw up, allows me the option to "fix it in post[-production]." I've got nowhere to hide. It's happening *now*. I don't want Marie Osmond fainting at my feet while I'm daydreaming about where I'll grab a drink after the show.

Live television, like life itself, gives you only one shot. It's a good idea to pay attention.

3

DULCET TONES AND HIDDEN GIN

I T WAS A SUNDAY AFTERNOON IN 1974. I WAS MIDWAY THROUGH MY four-hour shift as the board operator on WHAV-FM. "Bored" operator was more like it. The mind-numbing track from an album by 101 Strings, an elevator-music rendition of "Hey Jude," was mercifully coming to an end. It was time for me, now an eighteen-year-old full-time broadcaster, a one-year veteran, to muster my most dulcet tones and pause for station identification. *If* I could emerge from my stupor.

While WHAV's AM station mostly featured Top 40 hits, the FM side was a "beautiful music" format. To me, it was neither beautiful nor music. More like audio chloroform. This stuff would get you into REM sleep faster than a lecture on the Dewey decimal system.

I flicked the toggle switch and turned the dial, all traces of the old heart-thumping anxiety gone. Then, in a practiced voice both saccharine and serene, I ratted out the guilty party in these crimes against music.

"The new wave is rolling in, ninety-two point five stereo, WHAV-FM, Haverhill."

As I spoke, I stared at the words a previous announcer had scratched into the metal console with a knife edge or nail file: "The new wave is in your john."

Welcome to show business.

And I was in show business—sort of. Although I have to admit the bloom was already fading a bit. My high school friends had gone away to college. They were having sex, getting wasted, and, presumably, attending classes. I, on the other hand, was still in our hometown, in a room by myself, segueing Mantovani and Percy Faith records and occasionally schmoozing into an expensive piece of metal.

It was my own fault. I'd turned down a potential scholarship to Emerson College in Boston because, as I reasoned at the time, "Why should I leave a job in radio to go to school to try to get a job in radio?" No denying the logic. Hindsight is twenty-twenty, and from where I sit now, it seems I made the right choice. But back then, fresh from hearing my boss Ed Cetlin's admonition, "Tommy, just play the records and read the commercials. We're a no-personality station," I was beginning to feel like I'd made a really dumb call.

A "no-personality" station? What the hell was that? *How can you even* have *no personality?* The whole reason I'd dreamt of a radio career since I was in grade school was *because* of personalities. People like Jean Shepherd from New York's WOR (best known for the film version of *A Christmas Story*), whose intricate, hypnotic stories I'd listen to way past my bedtime while hiding under the covers with my transistor radio. And Larry Glick from Boston's WBZ, who years later would become a real friend, but whose mischievous on-air antics made him always feel like one. These were my heroes, my inspiration. I was supposed to be their *complete opposite*? As indistinct and forgettable as the music I was playing? As memorable as an elevator ride? What would some kid be inspired to do after listening to *me*?

"After hearing Tom Bergeron on the radio, I decided to go off and watch paint dry."

I couldn't do it. I couldn't just surf "the new wave" into Anonymity Cove. But I didn't want to get fired. It was one thing to be a working broadcaster envious of his friends away at college; quite another to be an unemployed teenager whose nascent career had self-destructed. That would be a disaster. But I needn't have worried. Help was on the way from several unlikely circles.

The red button on the multiline studio phone began to blink silently. Usually that meant the boss was calling. And if the boss was calling, that could mean anything. Once I received a call from him because he wanted me to stop playing Streisand. "No female vocals," he decreed. Another time he was at a party and wanted me to play more up-tempo music. Like the radio station was his private jukebox. Which, in essence, it was. But it was doubtful he'd be partying this early on a Sunday afternoon. Frankly, the image of him partying at all was hard to imagine. Creepy, even, to my eighteen-year-old self. It couldn't be that he was calling because I'd invested too much personality into my "new wave is rolling in" delivery. I was sure I'd sounded convincingly like a pod person. All of my speculating hadn't stopped the red light from blinking, so I punched the button and answered the phone.

"FM studio, Tom here," I said.

There was good news and bad news. The good news: it wasn't the boss. The bad news: it was the police.

"There's something wrong with your AM station," the officer informed me. "We've been getting calls."

"Really?" I said. "No kidding. What about?"

"It's off the air. Has been for about twenty minutes. You haven't received any calls?"

"Um, no, not that I noticed," I answered.

I lied. I'd seen the yellow lights blinking, but I'd ignored them. The way I figured it, who would be calling the FM station? It wasn't likely an army of 101 Strings fans were jamming the lines with song requests. And if such an army, or even a misguided platoon, actually existed, I definitely wanted nothing to do with *them*.

"I'm hearing a clicking sound on the air, but that's it," the officer said.

The FM studio had a soundproof-glass window on the far wall through which you could see the production studio and, on the other side of that, through another window, the AM studio. I peered through the glass and was sure I could see the massive body of the AM announcer, the spitting image of Peter Griffin from *Family Guy,* with his feet up on the counter by the microphone. He was host of a big-band show on Sunday afternoons—or at least he had been until about twenty minutes earlier.

"Let me check it out," I said. "I'll call if there's a problem." *Like if he's dead,* I thought with a shudder.

We hung up, and, after a seamless transition to the latest Henry Mancini offering (first things first), I made my way through the empty newsroom and up the narrow stairs to the AM studio. Even before I got there I could hear the snoring. Once I did get there I could smell the sweat and booze. He wasn't dead. He was just dead drunk.

The AM studio was small, and, in the face of the sensory assault, it seemed a lot smaller. Still, Henry Mancini and the Haverhill Police Department wouldn't wait forever. I angled past him to the turntable, lifting the needle that was clicking away at the end of the album's tracks. After turning the record over, I placed the needle back down at the start of the first tune. As the Glen Miller Orchestra returned to the airwaves, I leaned over Snoring Beauty's legs, coming way too close to his way too smelly feet as I reached for the microphone switch. The trick, if I could avoid sudden asphyxiation, would be to time a station ID between his snores.

I almost made it. "1490 AM, WH—" I said, before a massive, full-throated snort boomed from behind me. "—AV," I finished, adding, "Time at the tone, 2:14." I made sure to say it with no personality.

I returned to the AM studio a few more times that afternoon, changing albums and playing recorded jingles, until finally, from the FM side, I saw the AM announcer through the window as he suddenly sat up. It was quite the sight. He wasn't exactly the poster boy for coordination. His entire body mimed *What the fuck!?!* before he settled down and resumed playing the big-band sounds, probably at low volume. If he suspected I had kept the show going in his inebriated absence, he never mentioned it. And I never said anything to him. As far as he knew, it was a radio miracle.

To me, it was a radio mystery. He had been absolutely blotto, passed-out drunk, and yet I hadn't seen a bottle, a glass, a nip, or anything else incriminating in the studio. Somehow, between the times I waved to him as my shift began and when I received the call from the police department almost two hours later, he'd been drinking. A lot. It wasn't until a few days later, when I expressed my befuddlement to one of the newsmen (in complete confidence, of course; radio people *never* gossip), that I got my answer.

"He hides it back here," the intrepid reporter said as we walked to the back of a floor-to-ceiling metal console, which held the transmitter monitors. It was situated directly behind the AM studio. That made it easier for the on-air staff to take the required meter readings. And, I was about to discover, to stash their booze.

He opened the thin metal access door, stepped back with a dramatic flourish, and sang, "Ta-da!" Inside, on a small shelf next to the back end of a monitor, were several bottles, one almost empty. There was some gin, some whiskey, and not quite as much vodka.

"Wow," I said as I looked at the makeshift minibar.

"Wow indeed," the newsman replied.

And then I had a thought; a thought that began, hallelujah, to lead me toward the light. It wasn't, *How sad, Snoring Beauty is clearly an alcoholic* or *How dare he be so unprofessional as to use so much booze and so little deodorant?* Instead, the thought I had as I surveyed his stash was *This guy is a character. And if there's one thing a character has, whatever else he might be lacking, like a functioning liver, it's a personality.*

It wasn't quite an epiphany. I still didn't have, nor would I for some time, a handle on exactly *who* I was when I opened the microphone. Sure, I wasn't really nervous anymore. The terror and tunnel vision were gone. But I'd only replaced them with a bland acquiescence. And that, more than getting fired, was true self-destruction.

What I started to appreciate, the boss's edict notwithstanding, was that this wasn't a "no-personality station." This place was *oozing* personality. Jean Shepherd would have loved this crew. My intoxicated coworker was only one example. As the months passed, I became determined to learn things from these people, even if it was only what *not* to do.

Lesson: don't drink alone or within earshot of police headquarters.

There was the veteran Boston broadcaster, now mysteriously no longer employed there, who drove to Haverhill each Saturday night to host a single six-hour shift. He'd stroll into the studio carrying a portable black-and-white television set, which he'd watch for the entire six hours, showing less interest in the radio shift than in the bargains he'd stumbled upon at the supermarket.

"Can you imagine getting four cans of peas at that price?" he'd asked me one time, with all the enthusiasm of a child on Christmas morning. "I hate peas, but I couldn't pass that up."

Lesson: develop outside interests, even if you can't stomach them.

There was the announcer, let's call him "Ears," who'd have lunch in the production studio used for the nightly talk show and would, by manipulating the control board, eavesdrop on everyone's private phone calls. I'll admit it: sometimes I joined him. One such call involved a frustrated staffer grousing in dead seriousness about his daughter's recent behavior. "She doesn't need a psychiatrist," he pontificated. "It's all in her head." Another's extramarital planning sessions, complete with nauseating pet names, became our occasional lunchtime entertainment.

Lesson: it's not really nice to tap someone's phone or call them "My Little Love Rod."

There was the boss himself, who had turned the spacious downstairs room once designated by the original owners as the "Announcer's Lounge" into a storeroom for the neckties he sold to local businesses. This perceived indignity to the on-air staff did not sit well with one partially unhinged announcer. During his air shift, if he saw the boss descend the staircase toward Tie Central, he'd go on the air sounding like Bela Lugosi to proclaim that "Israel [the boss was Jewish] is counting his cravats." He'd say it loudly, *on the air,* and draw it out like a Shakespearean Dracula. Sometimes he'd say it between commercials; sometimes he'd boom the non sequitur right over a song.

"Izz-rye-al is coun-ting hizzz cra-VAHTS!"

That had to leave some commuters staring at their radios.

Lesson: find a healthy outlet for your frustrations, preferably one that's untraceable.

Then there was the staffer who eventually became the morning-drive host on the AM side. On that shift he'd spend seven hours a day, six days a week, in the cramped, dimly lit studio, alone—like veal with headphones. As a result, while he was gradually developing a glib, self-assured on-air personality, he was also developing a socially awkward, insecure off-air personality.

Lesson: whether your glass is half empty or half full, at least you have a glass.

That last guy was me.

I learned two important things during my first stint in radio: One, the person you should be when you open that microphone is *yourself.* And two, just because you know that first thing doesn't mean you can do it. Especially when you feel like the personality you're developing is a split personality.

I needed help. I needed a mentor. And I found one. But not until the boss threatened to fire me. And not until I looked in the most unlikely place. Because, as it happened, the best broadcasting teacher I ever had was . . .

A mime.

4

A MIME IS A TERRIBLE THING
TO WASTE

I WAS IN A SMALL ROOM. TRAPPED. AND, TO MAKE MATTERS WORSE, the walls were closing in on me. I leaned into one wall and then another, pushing against them with increasing desperation as my space and options diminished. Several feet away, an intense, compact critic named Tony Montanaro watched me struggle and shook his head.

"No, no, I'm not buying it," he said.

My arms dropped to my side. The invisible walls dropped away, too. *So much for my audition,* I thought.

"You're not Marceau," he continued, referring to the famous mime with whom he'd studied. "You're not built like him. Why are you trying to be Bip [Marceau's signature character]?"

I shrugged. I hadn't expected it to go like this. I thought I was pretty good. I wasn't alone, either. Applauding, laughing audiences back home had confirmed that I was pretty good. Hadn't they? Wasn't that what their reaction was telling me? But now, as I stood on the stage of this converted barn in South Paris, Maine, home of the Celebration Mime Theater, I felt like a hack. What was *this* guy's problem? Surely one of us was confused. And he wasn't named Tom.

"You can't be someone else," Tony said with a smile, his tone suddenly feeling more supportive than dismissive. The smile was instantly disarming, springing to his face like it belonged there and was eager to get back home. "Each of us has our own gifts. You have to find out who *you* are onstage."

He was right. That's exactly what I needed to do. I hadn't come up here (sorry, it's Maine; I meant "down here") to be a clone of Marcel Marceau. I'd decided to study mime in Paris (OK, *South* Paris) to find my own voice. Well, it's mime, so not my *voice* exactly, but . . .

OK, wait a minute. Maybe I should step back a bit. You may be wondering how I went from local radio in the last chapter to auditioning in front of a mime in this one. Fair enough. But stay with me; it all makes sense. Eventually.

As I said, it really started when the boss threatened to fire me.

It turns out I wasn't the only one conflicted about my passing up college to stay in radio. My boss, Ed Cetlin, was, too. Despite his gruff exterior, he'd developed a somewhat paternal attitude toward me. And, truth be told, I'd become fond, if still somewhat warily, of him. During one of his lunchtime eavesdropping sessions, "Ears" told me he'd heard Cetlin discussing me with a friend.

"He's a good kid," he'd said, according to Ears. "A bit of a hothead, but a good kid. But he's never going to make it in radio."

"Really?" I asked Ears. "He doesn't think I'm any good at this?" By now I was the AM morning-drive host, a job not usually given to an underachiever.

"He didn't say *that*. He just thinks you're a little rough around the edges or something. Don't worry about it."

Right. Your boss thinks you have no future. No worries at all.

It wasn't long afterward that the boss asked me to come into his office. He was sitting at his desk when I entered, and he invited me to take the chair across from it. I did. Then I waited a few seconds as he leaned back in his chair, squinted in my direction, and chewed one end of his glasses.

"Tommy, it's bad," he said.

I was confused. "It is? I am?"

He ignored my probing questions. "You can't just work *here*. Not at your age."

"I can't?" I was on a roll with the banter.

"I didn't hire you thinking you wouldn't go to college. I thought you'd work here for a while, get some experience, then go to school and continue your education."

I gave him my "Why leave a job in radio to go to college to get a job in radio?" rationale. He wasn't buying it.

"You do a good job here. You're a good kid. But if you don't at least take some college courses, you're fired."

I wasn't sure I'd heard him correctly. "You'll actually *fire me* if I don't go to school?"

"I will."

There it was, the ultimatum. Looking back on that day over thirty years later, it's still the most thoughtful threat to my job security I've ever received. Expand your horizons or I'll show you the door. Don't just settle. Grow or go. Even then I took it in the spirit it was given. I walked out of his office surprised but appreciative. He'd given me the kick in the butt (aiming right for the pocket with the wallet) that I was incapable of giving myself.

Now I had to decide where to go and what to study. To keep the morning shift and also go to school, my only realistic option was the local community college in Haverhill, Northern Essex. Parsing Cetlin's demand carefully (he didn't say I had to work toward a degree, for example), I decided to enroll only in courses that seemed like fun—the "classroom as dessert cart" approach.

One offering in particular caught my eye: a mime course. Nowadays, mimes are held in the same high regard as, say, game-show hosts. (What *is* it with my career choices?) But in the mid-seventies, before they'd managed to piss off millions of people in public parks, mimes were actually kind of cool. Marcel Marceau in particular.

Plus, they were a tangible link to the masters of physical comedy I'd loved since childhood. Jean Shepherd and Larry Glick may have been my radio heroes, but when it came to the movies I only had eyes for Buster Keaton, Charlie Chaplin, Laurel and Hardy, and, of course, the Three Stooges (the Curly years, thank you very much).

In fact, two of the Stooges, Moe (the bully with the bangs) and Larry (the frizzy-haired one), were the first celebrities I ever interviewed. I was sixteen. It would be another year before I would be working at the local radio station. I was home alone. My parents and younger sister were all out. It was just me, the telephone, and a crazy idea.

I wonder if I could reach Moe Howard and Larry Fine.

So, armed only with that impulse, and oblivious to long-distance phone charges, I dialed Los Angeles information.

"Do you have a listing for Moe Howard or Larry Fine?"

The operator checked. "We have several listings for M. Howard," she said when she returned, "but only one for Larry Fine."

"I'll take it!" I said.

I copied down the number and thanked her profusely before hanging up. Then, I affixed a small suction cup to the earpiece of the phone, plugged the attached cord into my tape recorder, took a deep breath, and called Larry.

His mother answered.

Math wasn't my strongest subject in high school, but with my knowledge of the Three Stooges' career, I estimated his mother's age at 114. The woman on the phone sounded 40.

"Oh no." She laughed. "My son isn't *that* Larry Fine. This happens a lot."

My heart sank.

"But I do know how you can reach him," she continued.

My heart pounded.

"He's at the Motion Picture Country Home in Woodland Hills."

After more profuse gratitude I continued the search. This time I hit pay dirt. The man who answered the Woodland Hills number was only too happy to go and fetch Larry. But when he returned moments later, he was Stooge-less.

"He's playing poker. Can you call back in half an hour?"

"Sure," I said. After all, it was my parents' phone bill.

When I called back, Larry came to the phone. He was recovering from a stroke and there was some impediment to his speech, but the nasal voice from all those films was unmistakable. He was charming. Within several-long distance minutes he'd put this nervous sixteen-year-old totally at ease. We talked about the history of the comedy team and how he'd met its other members. He could tell I was a true fan. "So do you want Moe's number?" he asked.

I couldn't believe my luck. At this rate I'd be talking to Charlie Chaplin by midnight. I took down Moe's number, and, after asking Larry if I could call him again sometime (he said yes, and I did), I moved on to my second Stooge. Moe, whose home number apparently was unlisted, wasn't as happy to have a kid cold-calling him.

"Who gave you this number?" he asked, sounding every inch the guy who handed out eye pokes and slaps to the skull.

"Larry did," I answered.

There was a brief pause. "Larry," he said. I imagined him shaking his head and thinking, "That lamebrain."

Whatever he was thinking, his tone changed from irritated, to resigned, to animated. The conversation truly became an interview, with Moe weighing in on everything from PTAs (he was annoyed they complained about the Stooges' violence) to residuals (they didn't receive any for the endless rebroadcasts of their short films). After I promised I'd protect his phone number, he said I could call him again, too (and I did).

I never did talk to Chaplin.

The mime course at the community college became, ironically, my ticket to stay in radio and my ticket to leave. On one hand, I avoided getting fired once I signed up; on the other hand, the class awakened a love for live performance that a radio studio couldn't satisfy.

Soon I was a member of the school's theater company. Within months, after finding I took easily to the study of physical comedy, I formed a mime trio with my professor, Gene Boles, and a talented, effervescent young woman named Debbie O'Carroll. We called ourselves Vaudomime, an awkward marriage of the words *vaudeville* and *mime.* One of our sketches was inspired by my growing interest in meditation and Eastern religions and the fact that I could easily twist my legs into a full lotus position. It was called "The Bogus Buddha." Playing a con man posing as a guru, I get stuck in the position while trying to flee from police. I hop, I flail, I walk on my knees. By the end I've locked both feet behind my head, rolling about onstage like a white-faced Weeble. Gene and Debbie come to the rescue, each hooking an arm under one of my legs and carrying me off like oversized luggage.

Within a year, Vaudomime had performed on several area campuses, in local theaters, and at summer festivals. We had fun, but for me, something was missing. For all the laughs and applause we received, I knew I was only getting by on my passable Dick Van Dyke and Marcel Marceau impressions. Like the bogus Buddha, I was stuck. On the radio I was stuck, too. I was developing a split personality due to countless hours alone in the studio. Despite growing confidence on the air, I was, in my personal life, flailing like my con man onstage.

I was quick with a quip but slow to open up. A great first date. Not so hot on the third. And now I had a strange split public personality, too: disc jockey by day, mime by night. That prompted one friend to point out, "When we hear you we can't see you, and when we see you we can't hear you." Even with my meager math skills, I counted three personalities too many. If Freud hadn't died I could have had him on retainer.

Gertrude Stein once said about her hometown, "There is no there there." The same was true not of Haverhill, but of me. Peel away the stage impressions and the snappy patter, and I wasn't sure who was left.

I was in a small room. Trapped. And, to make matters worse, the walls were closing in on me.

It was time to get out of Dodge.

5

I'LL ALWAYS HAVE
(SOUTH) PARIS

I WAS IN A BATHTUB IN A ROOMING HOUSE IN THE MIDDLE OF A HEAT wave. The humidity was around 200 percent. My small attic living space had gathered all of the hot air from the house's lower floors and was holding onto it tightly despite the whirring fan in the sole open window. I'd attempted to nap, but then, afraid I might actually burst into flames, I'd gone downstairs to the communal bathroom to stretch out in a tub of ice-cold water. Maybe, I thought, a cramped, dimly lit, *air-conditioned* radio studio wasn't so bad after all.

Hindsight. What a bitch.

My audition for Tony Montanaro had been a success—sort of. He'd agreed to let me study at his theater, but not with him. I was offered an apprenticeship with one of the members of his company. What that meant was I could move to South Paris, Maine, find a place to live, and, whenever he could squeeze me in, pay for a class with one of Tony's former students. It wasn't ideal, but I was sure it would work. At least I *thought* I was sure. More or less.

I'd learned about Tony and his school at precisely the time I'd been desperate for a sign of what my next step should be. I'm agnostic, so I'm not big on the whole "divine intervention" thing, but I was *more* than happy to make an exception in this case. There are no atheists in foxholes and no agnostics in career funks.

Interestingly, the thought of finally going to one of the colleges that the friends I envied still attended never occurred to me. If it had, I'm sure I would have quickly dismissed it. Me become a freshman at almost twenty-two years old? Why, that would have been crazy. So, *not* being crazy, I instead went off by myself to study mime in a converted barn in the Maine woods.

And I hated it. Not the occasional classes; those only whetted my appetite for more. My teacher, Fateh Azzam, had been born in Beirut, the child of parents who'd fled Palestine in 1948. He was a thoughtful, talented artist who years later became director of a human-rights organization based in Ramallah. In addition to being a fine teacher, he opened my eyes to a world beyond spinning records and honing Rob Petrie impressions.

What I hated was that I'd jumped the gun. I'd been impulsive, romanticizing the idea of going off to be an apprentice. I'd left Haverhill with a spring in my step and a song in my heart. But I ended up flying solo again, trading hours alone in a radio studio for hours alone in a town where I knew no one, orbiting a theater where I was welcome only a few hours a week. And did I mention it was *really* humid? I became a poster boy for self-pity. I had a sprung spring. But I also had a plan B. I'd come back when I could be part of a class, living in the dorm with other students, taught by Tony himself.

I returned to Haverhill and, thanks to a friend, got work at an afternoon latchkey program for elementary school kids in nearby Lawrence, Massachusetts. In addition, when he heard I was back in the area, Ed Cetlin made me an offer to return to the airwaves. It felt strange going back there after making such a big deal about leaving, but hey, this time I knew it was for a short time, and it sure beat a cold bathtub in a heat wave. For about seven months, I worked those two jobs and, by moving back home with my parents, stashed cash. Then, having enrolled in Tony's two-week spring session, I bade farewell to my hometown again and returned to South Paris. No spring in step or song in heart this time. This time I left with a clear head and a fat wallet. It worked out much better.

The two weeks turned into ten when, based on my work, Tony invited me to stay for the more intensive summer session. I was ecstatic. In that more advanced class we'd be working on individual and group pieces and, the best part, performing them each weekend for an audience of locals and tourists.

Remember when I said there were two things I learned during my first stint in radio?

One, the person you should be when you open that microphone is yourself. *And two, just because you* know *that first thing doesn't mean you can do it.* Or even *want to,* especially if the definition of "yourself" isn't all that clear yet.

But here, in the hands of a teacher who wouldn't tolerate my old, derivative parlor tricks, I was beginning to find (no mime pun intended) my voice.

Tony's ability to spot even the slightest false note in a performance never ceased to amaze me. It's one thing for a director to stop you for not doing it his way. It's quite another for a director to stop you for not doing it your way—for lazily drifting into old tricks designed to get easy laughs or applause. What I learned from him then I've used onstage, on radio, on television, and in my life ever since. Find your center. Be present. And risk failure (which is subjective, anyway).

Years later, in 2002, long after I'd married, become a father, and gone to work in Hollywood, I was on vacation in Portsmouth, New Hampshire, having breakfast with a friend. My cell phone began buzzing. It was Tony. Despite the passage of time, his voice hadn't lost any of its youthful energy and enthusiasm. And, although we hadn't seen each other very often during those years, I hadn't lost the feeling of being his student. What he thought about what I did always mattered to me.

"Karen and I were watching *America's Funniest Home Videos* last night," he said, referring to his wife and performing partner. "You were in the audience with the woman who laughed at everything you said."

Although I'd taped that show months earlier, I remembered it vividly. From the stage I'd spotted a woman who, despite being stone-cold sober, thought everything I did was hilarious. As we were about to shoot my next clip introduction, I asked our director and executive producer, Vin Di Bona, if he'd just follow my lead. I wanted to try something. "Sure," he said. "Go for it." *AFV,* unlike the live *Dancing with the Stars,* is a taped show. If it didn't work, it would never air.

I moved into the audience and plunked down next to my giddy fan. Then, because her reaction to everything was so big, so out of control, I became almost still and completely in control. Ms. Yang, meet Mr. Yin. I gazed at her stone-faced, as if placidly examining a science experiment. This only made her laugh more. When she'd stop, only the slightest gesture, like tipping my head to her shoulder, would start the cascade again.

"You played it perfectly," Tony said. "We loved it. I had to tell you."

I felt like I'd just won an Emmy®. "I learned it from you," I said.

He laughed. We talked a bit more, giving each other brief updates on our lives. I sent my love to Karen and he sent his to my wife, Lois, and our daughters. Before we hung up I said, "This really meant a lot to me, Tony. Thanks."

In December, after I returned home to Connecticut following an *AFV* taping, Lois gave me the mail that had accumulated in my absence. Sitting on the floor in my office, I separated the bills from the Christmas cards. The bills could wait. I wanted to open the cards, especially the one with the Casco, Maine, return address—the one from Karen and Tony Montanaro.

It wasn't a Christmas card. It was a note from Karen, along with copies of some newspaper stories. Obituaries. A death from cancer.

Tony Montanaro. Born September 10, 1927. Died December 13, 2002.

I wept. I was totally present. He would have liked that.

6

SOMETIMES A LOW ROAD
IS A HIGHWAY

W E'VE ALL SEEN NEWS STORIES STARRING MEGA LOTTO WIN-
ners as they grip massive cardboard checks and smile like deer hypnotized by the headlights of an oncoming train. On one hand, you
can't help but feel a little envious. After all, they've just won more
money than Bill Gates makes in an afternoon. Then again, you can't
help but feel a little smug, either. You know what's probably coming
next. Fast-forward one year, and each member of the once-happy
couple has a high-powered lawyer and the homicidal glares that *only*
money can buy.

Which brings me to a story. It's one of my favorite Zen fables.

There was once a wise old farmer who owned a prize horse.
One day his horse ran away. Upon hearing the news, his neigh-
bors came over to offer their condolences. "Such bad luck," they
said sympathetically. "Maybe" was all the farmer replied. A
few days later the horse returned, bringing with it three other
wild horses. "How wonderful," the neighbors exclaimed.
"Maybe," replied the old man again. The following day, the
farmer's son tried to ride one of the untamed horses, was thrown
off, and broke his leg. Once again, the neighbors offered their
sympathy, saying, "How awful." "Maybe," answered the farmer

one more time. The day after that, military officials came to the village to draft young men into the army. Seeing that the son of the farmer had a broken leg, they passed him by. The neighbors once again congratulated the farmer on how well things had turned out. "What good *fortune," they said. The farmer replied yet again, "Maybe."*

I think the moral of this story is pretty obvious. *If you're looking for scintillating conversation, forget about wise old farmers.*

The *other* moral, of course, is that it's pretty hard to know for sure whether the pile of poop you're standing in contains a pony. You might be having good luck and, after some digging, ride off into the sunset. Or, you might just be standing in poop. Without a shovel and a little perspective, it's really hard to tell.

For me, the period between the fall of 1978 and the spring of 1980 was like that. Ultimately, I found a pony, but at the time it more often felt like a steaming pile of . . . well, you get the idea.

I left South Paris, Maine, and Tony's class late in the summer of '78 with renewed enthusiasm and a fresh approach. No longer was I an *extremely* pale imitation of Marcel Marceau. No more whiteface makeup. No more dual personalities in my work. With Tony's help and encouragement, I'd found a creative intersection between radio and the stage. One sketch I wrote, *The New Adventures of Pinocchio,* is a perfect example. It involved the famous marionette becoming a real little boy only after winning a disco dance contest. (Yes, a disco dance contest.) *Saturday Night Fever* had been released the previous December, and John Travolta was a freshly minted superstar. The film was still playing in Maine theaters that summer, and I went several times, notebook in hand, to try to write down, in the dark, what I could remember of his dance steps. Then I set out to adapt his footwork for a wooden, strung-out version of Tony Manero.

Unlike my previous sketches pre-Montanaro school (yes, PMS), this one would utilize my radio training, too. I called WHAV and, with a quick OK from my former boss, drove to Haverhill to get to work in a production studio. I recorded a comedic narrative track, mixed Bee Gees music for the climactic dance, and brought the whole package back to the theater. That weekend, after several days of classroom workshops, I took to the stage in front of the paying crowd.

As the sketch began, with my recorded voice seemingly recounting only the familiar fairy tale, my onstage Pinocchio moved about wistfully, hoping only for a day when his body would be flesh and blood. Then, in a departure from the original story, he learns that the answer to his dreams resides in a dance hall under a mirrored disco ball. He goes to the competition, his name is called, and suddenly the chart-topping sounds of the Bee Gees fill the air.

The audience response was explosive. A sound wave of laughter and applause smacked me right in the chest. I glanced briefly toward the wings and saw Tony beaming. I began to dance, each familiar movie move now seemingly being manipulated by an unseen Geppetto. Of course Pinocchio wins the competition and, to the accompaniment of *How Deep Is Your Love,* transforms before the audience into a real little boy.

I left the stage to actual foot stomping and cheers from the audience. I'd never in my life experienced anything like it. As I got to the wings, my classmates shook my hand and slapped my back in congratulations. The audience was still cheering. I walked back onstage and, both delighted and dazed, took a bow. As I returned to the wings a second time I remember thinking, "How the hell am I going to top *that?*"

In some respects, careerwise anyway, it would take twenty-seven years and another dance competition with decorative mirror balls for me to find out. That summer, however, I *couldn't* top it. Heaven knows I tried. The audience reaction was an addictive high, and I wanted another hit. But the more I tried, the less interesting the sketches became. As I learned pretty quickly, it can be a short hop from inspiration to desperation. Once I became hungry for that ego nourishment, I stopped enjoying the "now" of the work. I wasn't interested in the process any longer. I was too busy chasing after the applause.

The Pinocchio sketch was a labor of love at each step, from the original idea all the way to that first performance. The audience going bonkers was a sweet, unexpected bonus. In much of my other solo work that summer I was so fixated on achieving a similar outcome that I left my muse in my other suit and rushed my way through rehearsals. It was like I was frenetically trying to plan my own surprise party. The other sketches weren't horrible (OK, maybe that one about the insurance adjuster); they just weren't as much fun.

Several of us who'd become friends in Tony's class decided prior to leaving Maine to start a theater company in Amherst, Massachusetts. By combining our solo and group sketches we had a readymade show. The area colleges provided a ready-made audience. All we needed was a name. After much heated debate and cold draft beer, we settled on *The Amherst Mime Theater.* We pooled our resources and rented a house. By mid-August we'd set up shop and booked several performances.

By month's end I had the nightmare.

Imagine the wheel on *Wheel of Fortune.* Then imagine that instead of dollar amounts on the wheel there are coffins. In each coffin is one of your friends. No family members, just friends. You can't see their faces, although each coffin is open. You don't have to see their faces. You know that they're there. The wheel is spinning. Before it stops, before you know which face will suddenly become clear to you, you wake up.

I'd never had a dream like that before. I've never had one like it since. I'm not superstitious; I don't really believe in psychic phenomena or paranormal hocus-pocus. In that respect I am, truly, a doubting Thomas.

But then I received a phone call from home. On September 1, 1978—a day, maybe two, after I'd had the dream—a drunk driver killed a friend as she was driving home from Boston. Her name was Justine. She was twenty-two. She wasn't a close friend—more an acquaintance really, although I'd occasionally hoped to change that. She was a photographer for the *Haverhill Gazette,* and I'd met her when she showed up to cover a talent show I was hosting. I developed an instant crush. We'd kept in touch, a letter here and there, while I was away in South Paris. Nothing romantic, just friendly, but, to my way of thinking, a good start. Suddenly, tragically, she was gone.

I returned home for the wake. While I was there, Justine's mother told me she'd found one of my letters in her daughter's room. Here she was, in the midst of dealing with a parent's worst nightmare, comforting *me.* It was a kindness I'd be even more amazed at after becoming a parent myself. Not that I could envision myself in that role at the time. I couldn't even handle a casual romance, let alone a serious commitment. I was still a great first date, not so hot on the third. If a woman was initially attracted to me because of my sense of humor, she soon found it a frustrating barrier to any real intimacy.

Justine's death forced me to acknowledge that despite my growth as a performer, I still hadn't gotten much better at connecting as a person. In truth, even my letters to her had been performances. They contained glib substitutes for real emotions. While Tony's training had certainly been good medicine, I was still suffering from a split personality.

Not long after the funeral, I left Amherst for good. What seemed like a great idea while we were eager students in South Paris (*Let's start a theater company! Darla can make the costumes! Alfalfa can rent the hall!*) quickly lost its luster when we were entrepreneurial thespians in Amherst. Without Tony's guiding hand, we were on a rudderless ship, each of us eyeing the empty captain's chair. To mix metaphors, our boat had too many chiefs, not enough Gilligans.

Over the next sixteen months, I managed to be my own rudderless dinghy. In rather quick succession, I meekly returned to WHAV (again) and then, after several months, left (again) to crash with friends and try stand-up comedy in New York. I auditioned at several clubs and was hired by one (at no pay): the Magic Town House. I was the only nonmagician on the bill. My "act," such as it was, consisted of a lot of lame misfires and only one, all-too-true joke.

"Hi, I'm Tom Bergeron. I'm not really a magician. My job is to make the audience disappear."

It wasn't long before I was on a bus back to Newburyport, Massachusetts, and the apartment I was sharing with friends. I was broke. I was depressed. Ed Cetlin, tired of me treating his radio station like a financial pit stop, said no when I actually asked to come back (again). His response would prove to be as pivotal to me as his demand that I attend college.

The time in South Paris had been invigorating, but had dealt with only part of my sense of disconnect. I'd learned that it was possible (abortive stand-up career aside) to merge my stage and radio training into something that felt truer, less derivative. Absent any job prospects, however, and sinking into a swamp of self-pity, I had to start addressing some other areas. And fast.

There was once a wise guy who owned a high horse. One day, while up on his high horse, he fell off. Upon hearing the news, his family came by to offer their condolences. "Such bad luck," they said sympathetically. "Maybe" was all the wise guy replied. But then he added, "Although the pile of horse shit provided a soft landing. That's something."

Now I'd get to deal with Dr. Joker and Mr. Hide.

7

FROZEN DISHES, BOTTLED PIGS,
AND FLEXIBLE TUBING

I T WAS A WINTER MORNING IN 1979. I STAGGERED BLEARY-EYED into the kitchen of our triplex apartment, the vapor from my breath entering the room just ahead of me. In the sink was an assortment of dirty dishes. The day before (OK, maybe *several* days before) we'd left them there to soak. Now, however, they were encased in ice. We'd fallen a little behind in payments to the oil company (OK, maybe a *lot* behind), and they'd stopped their deliveries. The mercury had fallen, too. Bad combination.

I shared the rent (or had until running out of money) with a platonic female friend who'd gone off on vacation for a few weeks, leaving her ex-husband to look after their young son. He'd moved in to become primary parent for the duration. Our subzero version of *Two and a Half Men* wasn't going all that well.

I decided to brew some coffee (we still had electricity), but then I realized that although I could grind beans, there was nothing to pour onto them. Well, that's not technically true. There was *one* liquid in the house that hadn't frozen.

The formaldehyde.

On the kitchen table, in a sealed jar filled with the stuff, was a pig fetus. No kidding. A premature Porky was floating in formaldehyde a few feet from the frozen dishes. My roommate Leslie's ex was a science teacher, and he'd brought this little piggy all the way home from class.

Taking in the scene as I fought off hypothermia, I had a comforting thought: *Someday I'll look back on this moment and laugh.* Maybe.

One of the strangest freelance jobs I took during this period was as a glorified carnival barker at a trade show in Chicago. A local booking agent named Tommy Tucker (really) dangled a five-hundred-dollar payday in front of me if I could learn a series of rope tricks in six days and then travel to the Windy City. His original act had bailed and he turned to me as a last resort, hoping to save his commission. We were both desperate, so already we had something in common. Theoretically, once in Chicago, I'd stand in a small display area in a massive convention center using prestidigitation to dazzle passersby into buying whatever product I was pitching.

Let's consider this for a moment. Me, an undernourished, week-old magician, competing with neighboring displays featuring incredibly fit, bikini-clad models and getting *five hundred bucks* for it? Sign me up.

I should confess I have absolutely no memory of what company I worked for in Chicago. Not a clue. Don't even remember any of the rope tricks. I only remember that, too broke to buy appropriate clothes for the gig, I wore brown corduroys, an open, wide-collar shirt, a denim vest, and sneakers. The rest is a muddle—probably because it was too embarrassing (or maybe because of the hypothermia).

Several months later, having blown through my five hundred dollars like it was, well, five hundred dollars, I was sitting in the outer office of a factory in Haverhill's Ward Hill Industrial Park, filling out a job application. There was a box labeled "Salary Desired." That was where, in essence, they wanted me to assess my self-worth. Rather than indulge my prospective employer, I simply wrote, "Yes." It made me laugh. I dropped the unfinished application into the wastebasket and walked out. In that moment, despite leaving the building as unemployed as when I'd entered it, I knew things would be OK. My sick sense of humor was intact, and, as prescribed in the cliché, it was administering the best medicine.

Still, I was laughing all the way to an empty bank account. I needed a job. And I found one. Not at a radio station or in a factory. My first weekly paycheck in months, which I remember caressing like it was a lover's skin, came from a company in nearby Amesbury, Massachusetts. They made flexible tubing. And, for three whole months, I was one of their customer-service representatives. However, as it turned out, I was to customer service what the Hindenburg was to air travel.

The company no longer exists. I blame myself.

It wasn't intentional. It's not like I didn't try. I liked these people. I was grateful to be working again and paying down my debts. I was just really, really bad at it. I had the engaging-phone-skills part down pat. If you were looking for flexible tubing and I answered your call, my tone suggested bedrock dependability. That is, until I lost your paperwork.

And here's the irony. Even though I was completely unsuited for the job and quickly knew it, I was the happiest I'd been in over a year. I was no longer Sulky Stewart, captain of the Woe Is Me Express. I had, after that epiphanous laugh in the industrial park, charted a new course. I was now Possibility Pete, captain of, among other things, Nauseating Analogies.

One laugh. That's all it took to snap me out of a funk that made Eeyore look like a party animal. Down there, under all the sighing and self-loathing, there was still a snarky spark. I seized on it and began playing offense. The way I figured it, even if I was only stumbling forward, I was still heading in the right direction.

It was then, as I was lowering the bar for the customer-service profession, that I decided to give radio another try. Not at WHAV. That revolving door had mercifully been locked shut. This time I'd head north, about fifteen miles north, to Portsmouth, New Hampshire.

One problem: I didn't have a résumé. But this was the new me. I wasn't going to just type up a stale chronology of my experience. My résumé would be different. My résumé would *pop*.

It was going to be a cartoon.

I'd been a serious comic-book collector as a kid. Growing up, I spent hours alone (sensing a trend here?) sketching my own super-hero ideas. Over time I became a passable cartoonist—a hobby that, during my local-radio years, enabled me to occasionally sell free-lance editorial cartoons to the daily *Haverhill Gazette* and the weekly *Haverhill Independent*. Much later, when I became a father, I'd draw cartoons for my daughters before heading off to early-morning radio or TV show duties. The cartoons, which they'd find on the kitchen table while they were getting ready for school, always starred carica-tured versions of them and reflected things happening in their lives at the time. Well, always starred them until they reached puberty, that is. Then the starring role went to the cat. I found it incredibly difficult to draw my daughters with breasts, and they complained I was making them look too fat. The cat, who never complained, be-came the new headliner. But all that was yet to come. At this point in the story I was single, unemployed, and determined to stand out from the crowd.

Looking back, I'm amazed I got a job out of this. Here's what I did. I drew a caricature of myself, in full white-faced mime attire, leaning on thin air with a large word balloon on the page to my right. In the word balloon the *mime* Tom "talked" about his career high-lights. Brilliant, eh? A cartoon mime talking about his broadcasting credentials.

And it worked.

Within days I received a call from Duncan Dewar, program di-rector at WHEB-FM in Portsmouth. He wanted to meet me, if only, he admitted, to see the person behind this bizarre résumé.

"So you were in radio?" he said as he perused the cartoon.

I sat across from him in his office. "Yes."

"And then you were a mime?"

"Sometimes both at once," I said. "Well, on the same day, I mean. I never did mime on the radio. Too much dead air."

"Smart," he said. "And now you work where?"

"I'm in flexible tubing."

He looked at me straight-faced. "Of course."

The meeting, believe it or not, went well enough to get me a weekend shift as a board operator during Casey Kasem's *American Top 40* program.

During the week I was the world's worst flexible-tubing rep, but on weekends I was once again working in radio. Sure, I was back to being a board operator, but this time I wasn't playing 101 Strings. This time I was counting down the hits with Casey.

"Keep your feet on the ground and keep reaching for the stars," he'd say to close each week's show.

I was ready to do exactly that.

8

THOREAU ANOTHER LOG
ON THE FIRE

URING MY MONTHS IN FUNKVILLE (NOT TO BE CONFUSED WITH Funky Town) I suffered from an acute case of tunnel vision. I'd have occasional sparks of perspective, a jolt of *Could we kindly get our head out of our ass?* inner tough love, but it didn't really help. My set point was self-pity, and that doesn't let in much light.

A popular pastime among several friends and me back then was to hang out at our favorite bar in Newburyport, the Grog, and piss and moan. We'd P & M about a wide variety of topics, but the favorite was (drum roll, please) *Nobody Really Gets Us.*

I know. Every generation thinks they invented that one. As George Costanza once put it on *Seinfeld,* "You can't use *It's not you, it's me!* I *invented* It's not you, it's me!" But guess what? You didn't. I didn't. My great grandparents didn't. *Nobody Really Gets Us* probably started with Adam and Eve, when there wasn't even anybody else to be nobody.

We'd drink beer and cry in it over the lack of appreciation society extended to its artistic youth (us, of course). Then we'd belch, nod approvingly at our own analysis, and order another round.

This went on for months. But, luckily, running on a parallel track in my life were conversations I was having with another friend, an area psychologist named Lee Wotherspoon. Although I definitely needed my head examined, I hadn't sought him out. His friendship was serendipitous. He'd shown up at a casting call for the Newbury-port Community Theater's production of *The Fantasticks* in early 1978. Not to audition. He'd decided to be a groupie, to shadow a pro-duction from its first day until its wrap party, which he graciously threw for us at his home.

I say "us" because I was cast as El Gallo, the swashbuckling lead. I'm a shade over five feet nine. The actor cast as the young boy was close to six feet. When I sang "Try to Remember," I was hoping he wouldn't forget to slouch.

Lee's impulse to be a groupie was completely in character for him. A former advertising executive for Gillette, he'd embarked on a new career after escaping a kidnapping attempt in Argentina during which his bodyguard was killed. Ransoming American executives was big business. Lee vowed he wasn't going to "get killed for razor blades." He became a psychologist, moved his family to New Eng-land, and began embracing life's other possibilities. As his practice was growing, so, too, was his checklist of adventures. *Hop a ride on a freight train?* Check. *Hitch rides with private pilots at airports?* Check. *Learn how a local theater works?* Check. If there was an experience to be had and it didn't conflict with his values—no breaking the law or bending his moral compass, for example—he'd have it.

Eventually I could see my parallel tracks diverging. On one track was the image of me at forty, imploding, still on the same bar stool drinking a pint of spoiled regret. On the other track was an expansive me with my own checklist, drinking from a glass that was always half full. It didn't take much time to decide which track to follow.

If you hold your breath, you lose it.

Lee's friendship, along with my love for the work of Thoreau, Steinbeck's *Travels with Charley,* and the first two seasons of *Kung Fu* (I really think they lost focus in the third) inspired me yet again to roll the dice and hit the road. This time, however, I wouldn't be leav-ing the radio job behind. I'd be taking it with me.

I pitched an idea to WHEB for an almost five-week series I called "The Month Across America." I explained that I'd travel from New England to California by hitching rides on planes, trains, and automobiles and file three reports a week from the road. The reports would feature the places I visited and the people I met.

They went for it. They agreed to pay me a stipend and provide me with a return ticket at month's end from any West Coast airport.

I'd left the flexible-tubing job by this point, my resignation accepted with palpable relief. They'd been too nice to fire me, but I'm sure they also would have paid me to go hop a train.

The timing for the trip was perfect. Professionally, I felt reenergized. Personally, another romance was ending badly. (Details of the latter will be available in the chronicle of my love life, *Much Ado About Nothing,* providing my lawyer can clear the title.) Preparing for the trip wasn't that difficult, despite the fact I'd quit Boy Scouts as a tenderfoot and had gone camping only once before. I'd often fantasized about embarking on just such an adventure, the radio reports being the only new addition, so the actual process of assembling the necessary items felt strangely familiar. On my back I'd carry a pack with, among other things, clothes, a sleeping bag, a tent, a tape recorder, and some cookware. In my pocket I'd carry a letter of introduction from Cliff Taylor, WHEB's general manager, confirming that I was indeed doing a radio series for him and wasn't just randomly annoying the locals.

At its essence, "The Month Across America" would be like one of Tony's improvisation exercises back in South Paris. Only three points would be certain: I'd know the character I was playing (in this case, *me* in the role of *me*), where I was starting from (outside my apartment in Newburyport, Massachusetts), and where I would end up (most likely in San Francisco). Everything in between would be, in the truest sense of the word, improvised. There would be no familiar daily routines to rely on. I'd have no idea on any morning where I'd be sleeping (or *if* I'd be sleeping) that night. From the moment I first extended my thumb toward oncoming traffic, I would be surrendering to the possibilities of the present moment.

As fifty-three-year-old Tom writing now about twenty-five-year-old Tom, it's easy for me to connect dots that I was oblivious to back then. The idea to become a hitchhiking radio host originated from the same source that pushed me to meditate and that needed to find a teacher to challenge me the way Tony did.

Years earlier, my WHAV boss, Ed Cetlin, had thrown down a gauntlet when he threatened to fire me if I didn't attend college. *Expand your horizons. Don't just settle. Grow or go.*

Remember the first thing I did when he said that? I parsed his ultimatum to see how much I could avoid acting on it. But, apparently *(light dawns on Marblehead)*, I was picking up that gauntlet in spite of myself. In incremental steps, with each decision, I was stumbling in the right direction just as I'd hoped. It was as if my subconscious had its own radio show and was broadcasting at a frequency that got through only to dogs and the thin section of my skull.

This is Radio Free Tom, brought to you by a grant from Get Your Ass off That Barstool Productions. I'm your host, Your Subconscious.

Joining me today are two people who couldn't be more different. One is a broadcasting veteran who has recently returned to radio following stints in theater and flexible tubing. The other is an emotionally guarded loner with periodic anger issues. Their names are Tom Bergeron. So tell me Tom, are you looking forward to what's ahead?

Me? Are you asking me? First, I'm *not* emotionally guarded. And I don't have periodic anger issues. That really pissed me off.

Sorry. Actually I was asking the other Tom.

I'm very excited, yes. This hitchhiking trip is a metaphor.

How so?

Oh, please. This is such a crock.

Again, I'm asking the other Tom.

Thank you. As I was saying, the trip represents a maturing awareness that life's riches are to be found when one embraces the "now" of life. Being fully aware of where you are makes the question of where you're going much easier to answer.

I see.

Who do I have to kill to get a beer around here?

Unfortunately, Tom, we're out of time.

You didn't ask *me* anything.

I've only got fifteen seconds. Say whatever you'd like.

Oh, sure, put it all on me. Typical. The hell with it, you wouldn't understand anyway. Nobody really gets m—

And good night.

9

HOPPING PLANES
AND ACHIEVING ORBIT

T HE STAR STATION ORBITING NORTHERN NEW ENGLAND." THAT was the slogan at the center of WHEB-FM's promotional campaign in 1980. Upon my return from "The Month Across America," I was offered a chance to be one of the station's five space cadets. My shift would be weeknights from seven to midnight. And because the ratings in that time period had blown a few heat shields, management generously let me rewrite the flight plan.

None of this would have happened if the hitchhiking series had tanked. But it didn't. From the first day I hitched a ride to the last, when I boarded a plane in San Francisco to fly back to Boston, the trip felt guided by an unseen hand. I rode with traveling salesmen, newlyweds, and truckers. I went to private-pilot terminals hitching rides across the Great Lakes with an aviation attorney and from Seattle to northern California with an empty-nest couple who invited me to spend the night in their home. I pitched my tent behind churches and on the embankment alongside a highway. I slept in warm beds after home-cooked meals and in my cold tent after dining from a vending machine. There were a couple of tense situations and a few pleasant flirtations.

In Whitefish, Montana, I spent the night on a park bench alongside the town's main street and was awakened by friendly policemen more interested in talking about my trip than sending me on my way. Later that day, in a bar on the same street, I downed boilermakers with a gregarious local who turned out to be the general manager of the Whitefish radio station. Between rounds, he offered me the station's morning-drive show. I passed. I had miles to go before I stopped. Plus, there was no guarantee he'd remember the offer when we both sobered up.

Through it all I had my microphone and tape recorder. I asked these people, these passing friends for a random day, to tell me about who they were and how they came to live their lives. I heard stories of dreams achieved and dreams deferred. I wrote in diners and filed reports on pay phones. WHEB's sales manager, Dick Rozek, relayed glowing reviews from listeners and clients back home. The trip had become everything I'd hoped it would be and more.

Apart from the scripts for the reports themselves, I kept almost no notes from the trip. No phone numbers or addresses of the people I met. No way to reconnect without hours of detective work and a lot of luck. That was by design. I wanted these brief connections to really matter in the present moment, in the "now" of them. I didn't want them diluted by the expectation of a "We'll have to get together again" platitude. In the way we always wish we'd said this or done that when someone we know suddenly dies, I wanted to be sure to say and do it right then. It became, in a sense, a moving meditation, and it established the foundation for everything good that's happened in my career since.

The fall of 1980 found me both comfortably settling into my new role as a nighttime DJ/talk-show host and hopelessly smitten with my new home of Portsmouth, New Hampshire. My body clock, after years of waking at 4:30 a.m. to host a morning show, took to my new nightly schedule like a well-rested duck to water. I was on the air from seven to midnight. I got to bed by two and slept as late as I wanted. Money was coming in. Debts were being whittled down. And, best of all, *I* was finally starting to "get me." As Dudley Moore said to Liza Minnelli in the film *Arthur,* after she said she'd never been on a yacht, "It doesn't suck." And it didn't.

The three years I did that radio show were a blast. It started out as a typical music show where I played records, took requests to play yet more records, and then read commercials before giving twice-hourly weather updates. (*Yawn.*) That format lasted about half of one evening. Still savoring the improvisational buzz of the hitchhiking series and given almost carte blanche by management to raise ratings, I decided to take a different approach. To arrive at the format revisions, I employed an extremely radical strategy brazenly developed without teams of consultants, reams of pie charts, or exhaustive audience research. It was bold. It was innovative. It was a no-brainer.

I turned the show into something *I'd* like to listen to.

From WBZ's Larry Glick in Boston (who would later become, and still is, a dear friend) I borrowed (or stole, or paid homage to) the concept of calling anywhere in the world when an offbeat news story caught my fancy. Usually these were stories well back from the front page, like the couple I interviewed after frozen human waste from an airplane toilet hurtled to earth from thirty thousand feet and flattened their woodshed.

"There was this big, blue chunk of ice in there. Made a hell of a noise," my telephone guest told me. "A couple of us picked it up and moved it. Now that I know what it was I wish I hadn't."

Or the bar in the Yukon where hearty souls downed a drink called "the sour-toe cocktail," a *really* dirty martini with the olive replaced by a frostbitten miner's dismembered human toe. Yummy. I called back after hearing that someone had accidentally swallowed the damn thing. They told me not to worry. They had more.

I invited area musicians to come into the studio and perform live. On several occasions, to raise money for local charities, I wrote sketch comedy shows that the whole staff and I performed as live broadcasts from the local theater. No more countless hours alone in a studio for me. This show was crawling with people, and I loved it.

And as an added treat, the ratings began to, appropriately, achieve orbit.

Thanks to Tony and my time in South Paris, I'd learned how to tap into my own performing instincts and apply them whether I was onstage or on the air. It was a lesson I'd have to relearn occasionally, but, like riding a bicycle, it would always come back to me. Eight years after my first radio show, and thanks largely to a mime, I'd begun to find my voice.

Quite often during this period I'd grab lunch at a dockside restaurant, the Old Ferry Landing, which overlooks the Piscataqua River and Portsmouth's working harbor. As I devoured a haddock sandwich, pored over newspapers, and jotted notes for that night's show, I'd inevitably be hypnotized by the view of the tugboats and the river's powerful current, the second fastest in the United States. Fall into that current, my friend, and you could quite easily be swept away. This is not to say that being swept away is always a bad thing. I was about to be swept away myself. But not by a powerful river.

By a redhead.

10

(MUCH) BETTER RED
THAN DEAD

I WAS CONVINCED THAT IT WAS A HORRIBLE IDEA.

Duncan, my program director, disagreed. "It'll be good for us. It'll be good for them."

Yeah, right. I was being asked to take my show on location, to broadcast from the studio of New Hampshire Public Television's annual fund-raising auction. Being out of *my* studio would completely mess with the show's rhythm. I couldn't see the upside.

"I won't be able to make any phone calls," I countered. "I won't have any place for guests."

"We'll set up a phone for you. We'll make sure you've got enough space for guests. It's only for one week."

He was being way too reasonable. I caved. How could I not? Duncan and Cliff, the station GM, had been consistently supportive. During one meeting in his office, Cliff informed me that my show's long-distance phone bill had almost eclipsed its ad revenue. I began to panic.

"I can't make any more calls?"

He shook his head. "No, keep making the calls. Just, if you like a story in Cleveland and a story in China, every so often go with Cleveland."

So, in the interest of team spirit, I set up shop in NHPTV's Durham, New Hampshire, studio. After all, what could possibly happen to the show in only one week?

To the show, as it turned out, nothing. To me, well, that's a completely different story.

There was once a wise-ass young radio host who had an increasingly successful show. One day his show was moved away. For a week. Upon hearing the news, his fellow DJs came over to offer their condolences. "Such bad luck," they said sympathetically. "Maybe" was all the young radio host replied. A few days later he did his show from the corner of a large television stage. "How wonderful," the radio station management said. "Maybe," replied the young radio host again. The following day, the young radio host noticed a hot redhead operating large TV cameras and occasionally barking good-natured orders at the TV crew. And she could swear like a truck driver. The young radio host was very intrigued. But every time he tried to make conversation with her, only inane blather escaped from his lips. She had never heard his radio show and, based on the evidence before her, thought him to be a dweeb. Once again, his fellow DJs offered their sympathy, saying "How awful." "Maybe," answered the young radio host one more time. The day after that the hot redhead, after being told by friends that the young radio host was really a nice guy, and feeling guilty she'd stonewalled him when he awkwardly tried to make conversation, invited him to join her and her coworkers for a drink after that night's broadcast. The voice in the young radio host's head congratulated him on how well things had turned out. "What good fortune," it said. The young radio host replied, "No shit, Sherlock."

I've been married to that hot redhead, Lois, my best friend, for twenty-six years and counting. We have two incredible daughters,

Jessica, who is now twenty, and Samantha, who is eighteen. And it almost never happened.

If *anything* underscores the Zen of my life, *this* does. Had Duncan acquiesced to my argument, to my negative expectation, I would have missed out on what continue to be the richest years of my life. And, on the career front, Lois wouldn't have been there to talk me out of my resistance years later when I was offered a chance to host a celebrity ballroom competition.

And you wonder why I meditate?

11

PHYSICS AND BLISS

Y THE MIDDLE OF 1982, I WAS A NEWLYWED. IT HAD BEEN A whirlwind courtship that caught us both by surprise. We'd each just come off bad breakups and hadn't been looking for another relationship, let alone a spouse. Within a year of our first date—a day shy of that anniversary, in fact—we were married. But with Lois working long hours as a producer at NHPTV and me now hosting a radio show and two TV shows (more about that in a minute), we'd decided to postpone our honeymoon until we could set aside enough time to really enjoy it. And that's just what we did when we finally spent a luxurious week riding horses and drinking mimosas in Santa Barbara, California.

Four. Years. Later.

We weren't procrastinating. We were just really busy. Of course, that's also the excuse I use for still owing thank-you notes to some of the wedding guests on my side of the family. That is, the ones who are still alive. Keep something on a to-do list for twenty-six years and there's a hell of an attrition rate. But as soon as I'm finished writing this book, I'm on it.

That week on location—the one I agreed to reluctantly—not only introduced me to my future wife but also started me on my television career. Another producer at New Hampshire Public Television, Chuck Tately, asked me to host a new magazine show soon to debut there called *New Hampshire Crossroads*. As Chuck had been my primary cheerleader in convincing a dubious Lois to give me another look, I quickly said yes.

One week. One laugh. Sometimes it doesn't take much at all to transform a life.

Chaos theory famously holds that when a butterfly flaps its wings in one area of the world, a hurricane can result hundreds of miles away. One action, seemingly irrelevant, can, with the right set of circumstances, create a major reaction. Although physics makes my head hurt, I'm a true believer. One thing I'd add in defense of the butterfly, however: sometimes its flapping doesn't create chaos. Sometimes it creates pure bliss.

One of my favorite memories is from the morning after my first date with Lois. The night before, she'd been in the front row of the audience at Theater by the Sea for the live broadcast of my sketch comedy show entitled "Monday Night Live." The show, a poke at how awful "Saturday Night Live" had become following the original cast's departure, was a fund-raiser for the theater and (he typed humbly) a sold-out smash. Afterward a group of us went off to a local bar for a celebratory drink or three. It was there, fueled by the inhibition-dulling effects of alcohol, that we had our first kiss. Or three. Early the next morning, unable to sleep, I walked from my studio apart-ment to Prescott Park on the bank of the Piscataqua River. I stood at the water's edge, deeply inhaling the salty morning air. It was late spring and the start of a perfect day. For the first time in my life I felt completely in balance. In my career as a broadcaster and performer I was firing on all cylinders, completely in the zone. In my personal life, where I'd too often been withdrawn and emotionally stingy, I suddenly felt wide open to the possibility of falling in love.

In our years together Lois has been as much an inspiration to the private Tom as Tony was to the public Tom. That's partly because she also worked in television and understands the demands of the business, but mostly it's because she, as we say in Massachusetts, is *wicked* smart about people. She certainly understands *me,* usually better than I do myself.

With her in my life, the split in my personality began to be mended.

Gotta love those butterflies.

12

LONG DAYS AND SHORT SPURTS

YOU WERE THE ONLY ONE WHO GOT OFF OF THE STOOL."

That's how Garland Waller, the producer on my *second* television show, explained to me how I'd won the job. The show was called *Super Kids,* a weekly magazine program for the six- to eleven-year-old set patterned after the then popular *Evening* (or in some markets *P.M.*) *Magazine.* I'd received a call at WHEB asking if I wanted to travel to Boston's WBZ-TV and audition for the host role. This after a previous call had invited me to audition to host a program called *Five All Night Live* at a competing Boston TV station, WCVB. The producer at WCVB didn't think I was right for *All Night,* but she did think I might be a good fit for the kids' show her friend was producing across town.

The audition for *Super Kids* went like this: I was escorted into a studio that was empty except for the several children sitting on the stage floor around a single stool. I was instructed to sit on the stool and was handed a paper bag.

"When we cue you," Garland told me, "just reach into the bag and improvise for the children with whatever you find in there."

Improvise? I thought. *Sweet.*

I waited for the cue and reached into the bag. I don't remember what was in it, but I do remember feeling awkward on the stool looking at the children craning their necks toward me. So, wanting us all to feel more comfortable, I got off the stool and sat on the floor with them. And, according to Garland, I was the only one among the hosting hopefuls who did.

The sudden flurry of phone calls offering TV auditions (if two constitute a flurry) came completely out of the blue. It turned out that among the listeners to my radio show were staffers at Boston's WCVB who lived in northern Massachusetts, well within WHEB's coverage area. They liked my show, so they talked about me with the *Five All Night Live* producer and, as the saying goes, "yadda, yadda, yadda."

So began a pattern that continues to this day, the "Let's see how many shows Tom can host at once" approach to career building. Each weeknight I continued my five-hour radio show from Portsmouth. On one weekday I'd be somewhere else in the Granite State shooting *New Hampshire Crossroads.* On Saturday I'd drive to Boston to shoot *Super Kids.* On Sunday it was back to WHEB for a three-hour afternoon shift. I also made myself available to WBZ to drive back to Boston during the week and fill in for their booth announcer whenever he took a day off as long as I could get back through rush-hour traffic to be on the air in New Hampshire that night. It was hectic, to be sure, but back then I was even younger than Ryan Seacrest. Younger than he is *now,* I mean. Back then Ryan was eight.

It's no wonder that during a visit with Lois's parents in Florida in 1982 I had a nightmare that I was stark naked and surrounded by microphones and cameras. Had I been an entrepreneurial visionary, I could have turned that nightmare into TMZ.com, the Web site whose sole purpose is to surround celebrities, the more naked the better, with microphones and cameras. Of course, like I said, it was 1982. I would have been waiting for someone to first invent Web sites.

Bob Lobel, another New Hampshire radio veteran, who spent years as WBZ-TV's star sports anchor, offered me some valuable advice when we both appeared on the New Hampshire Public Television Auction not long before my wedding to Lois. "You've got your foot in

the door," he said when I told him I'd been hired to host *Super Kids.*
"Make yourself invaluable. Whatever they offer you, take it."

And I did. By June of 1983, partly because I was exhausted, but
mostly so I could act on that advice, I reluctantly left WHEB and
New Hampshire Public Television to turn my full attention to Boston. I wanted to see just how far I could take a TV career that had
blown into my life on butterfly wings.

From the fall of 1981 until the spring of 1994 I was all over WBZ-
TV and, at various times during that span, WBZ Radio, too. I had my
foot in the door and my face on the tube. From *Super Kids* I went on
to host a weekly talk show with area high school students called *Rap
Around.* I cohosted specials on the growing threat of AIDS and the
ongoing threat of child sexual abuse. And, heeding Bob's advice,
when they offered me a job hosting the nightly state lottery drawings, I said yes.

Six nights a week for two years I was the guy who read the numbers on the balls that rolled into the little plastic trays. The daily
number just before 8 p.m. and the Megabucks number Wednesday
and Saturday just before 10 p.m. Taking the job was a calculated
risk. Everything else I'd been doing on the station, however noble
and high-minded, was scheduled either on low-viewership Saturday
afternoons or as prime-time cannon fodder against competing networks' hits. Every cockeyed optimist in the state of Massachusetts,
by contrast, watched the lottery drawings.

But, as with every calculated risk, there were pluses and minuses.
On the plus side, my face and name recognition skyrocketed, and I
managed to inject some touches of humor and personality into the
otherwise dry affair. "Welcome to *As the Wheel Turns,*" I'd announce
with mock gravitas. On Wednesday and Saturday I'd present the big-
money drawing clad in the penguin suit I referred to on air as the
"Mega Tux." On the minus side, when I was out in public, my role as
lottery host elicited some strange reactions. The best example was
when I walked into a funeral home in Haverhill for the wake of my

maternal grandfather. Another "mourner," whom I didn't know, actually yelled at me from the back of the place before I'd barely got past the front door, "Hey, Tom, can I rub your head for luck?"

Nice. Get out much, sir?

But the strangest thing that happened during my stint as lottery host was *my* fault. During those two years my live broadcast day really began each morning at 8:58, when I'd host the first of fifteen daily spots collectively called *4 Today*. Weaving between game shows and soap operas, I'd pop up with program notes, sixty-second interviews, and the world's shortest cooking segments. Actress Glenn Close actually promoted two movies with me in under a minute. When we were off the air she looked at me dumbfounded and asked, "What just happened there?"

Anyway, my point is that I had long days hosting short spurts. Sometimes that made for a foggy-headed Tom. Such was the case when I ended a daily lottery drawing one evening by encouraging the viewers to join us later for the Megabucks drawing. "Tonight's jackpot is three million dollars," I said to entice them.

The moment I was off the air several lottery officials (who were always on-set) surrounded me. They looked ashen.

"Why did you say that?" one of them asked.

"Say what?" I honestly had no idea what they were talking about.

"That the jackpot was *ten* million dollars!"

"Ten million? I said *three* million." These people were clearly nuts.

They held firm. They were really rattled. To calm them I brought them back with me to the tape room, where they could see the replay, hear me promote the proper jackpot amount, and then relax.

My smiling, dapper image appeared on the monitor. "Join us in two hours for *Megabucks Live*," I said. "Tonight's jackpot is ten million dollars."

Now *I* was ashen. I had just watched myself misstate the Massachusetts State Lottery payoff amount by *seven million dollars* and I had absolutely no memory of it. It was like being in a *Twilight Zone* episode where my body had been taken over by an alien invader with a lousy credit score. I could only imagine someone at the flexible-tubing company getting wind of this and saying, "See? This is what *we* put up with."

I apologized meekly on air during the *three*-million-dollar drawing, citing wishful thinking as the reason for my mistake.

That hiccup aside, those two years, during which time I also filled in regularly on the station's midday talk show, *People Are Talking,* gave management enough cautious confidence in my live TV skills for them to offer me the full-time job as *People Are Talking* host in 1987. Barry Schulman, WBZ-TV's program manager, had passed on offering me the job when it first became available in 1985, telling me I "looked too young."

By 1987 both of us had aged a bit. Certainly Barry had grown a few gray hairs as the result of my antics. Determined to make even a sixty-second appearance pop, I occasionally veered off in a comic direction too broad for Barry's taste. He'd cautioned my producer, Joel Rizor, and me one afternoon in his office. "Let's lose the slapstick, OK?"

We both acted suitably chastened, but we knew more trouble was on the horizon. While almost all of the *4 Today* spots were live, we'd pretaped one with a favorite guest: Legal Seafood head honcho Roger Berkowitz. Roger was promoting a charity auction where a bottle of wine from Napoleon Bonaparte's wine cellar would be up for bid. He'd carefully handed me the rare bottle, and I examined it reverently. However, just as the segment was ending and the *4 Today* logo was about to cover the screen, I pretended to lose my grip and bobbled the bottle. In the two seconds the logo replaced our image we dubbed in the sound of glass breaking followed by Roger's pained voice moaning, "Oh no." It was hilarious. And now it was exactly what we'd been told *not* to do. There was only one solution.

I hired a belly dancer to show up in Barry's office to distract him when it aired.

Absolutely true. And frankly, I'm still damn proud of myself.

13

NUTS, SLUTS, AND
HEADS OF STATE

THEY CALLED IT "NUTS AND SLUTS."

That was the in-house nickname for the show I'd inherited, known to the viewing public as *People Are Talking*. A daily, hourlong live talk show, *People Are Talking* aired on WBZ and several other Westinghouse stations in the 1980s and early '90s. On Baltimore's WJZ-TV, their *People Are Talking* was cohosted by Oprah Winfrey, who went on to become, as you may know, Oprah Winfrey.

The original host of the Boston version was Nancy Merrill. Later, Buzz Luttrell hosted the show, first with cohost Jan Jones and later by himself. For six years, from 1987 until its cancellation in June of 1993, I was its host. It was the Merrill version that had more of the Jerry Springer–like guest lists that earned it its nickname. Still, despite a newsier focus during Buzz's tenure and a more general-interest approach during mine, the name stuck.

I gave myself a nickname, "Donahue Jr." The format was almost identical to Phil Donahue's show. The budget wasn't. When our small studio audience was near full (usually around forty people), I could run around doing my "Donahue trot," fielding questions from them for our panel of guests. However, when the bus from the senior home broke down or the school field trip was canceled, resulting in dozens of empty seats, I'd bolt myself next to whatever warm bodies I could find so the camera wouldn't show the tumbleweed rolling by.

Still, full audience or not, it was a great gig. Every day was different. Every night I prepared for the next day's show like I was cramming for a final exam. Luckily, I was a quick study. After about an hour of reading the producer's pre-interviews and background information, I could hit the sack and let the information marinate during REM sleep. The next day on the air, armed with only minimal notes on an index card, I'd find myself recalling minute details and weaving them smoothly into the interviews. That discipline of quickly absorbing research, which I called "going into sponge mode," would serve me well years later when I filled in on *Good Morning America* and *The Early Show.*

In the interest of full disclosure, though, I must confess that my brain wasn't always sponge-mode worthy. This was particularly true during the period from 1990 to 1992, when, in addition to hosting the live, midday TV show, I also hosted the WBZ Radio morning show. From 5 till 9 a.m. I was on the radio, and then from 12:30 to 1:30 p.m. I was on live television. With that schedule, added to the fact that Lois and I were now the parents of two young daughters, sleep was a commodity in short supply. Occasionally, the seductive pull of slumber won out over my heavy-lidded attempts to slog through pre-interviews and background information for the next day's *People Are Talking.* This severely impeded my ability to smoothly weave minute details into the interviews. Truthfully, at my most fatigued, it severely impeded my ability to dress myself.

On such days I'd rely on the producer to hold up cards off camera that suggested questions or topic areas for me to pursue. They did this for every show. It was the talk-show equivalent of a pitcher/catcher relationship. When I was well rested I could glance over, read the card, and then either incorporate their suggestion or wave it off. When I was exhausted, I treated every card like a lifeline.

ASK ABOUT HER SISTER read the card on one of my sleepy days.

Her sister? I thought. *What sister?* My guest had been describing in emotional detail a harrowing experience that had changed her life. I think she was anyway. I was pretty tired. *I don't remember anything about a sister.*

I continued plodding along, hoping the stage manager would cue me to break for a commercial so I could confer with the producer. No such luck. He held up three fingers; three more minutes in this segment. In my mind I held up one. *Fuck.*

Once again the card appeared. ASK ABOUT HER SISTER.

Once again I ignored it. I could feel myself getting clammy.

Now my producer was almost apoplectic, waving the card insistently. ASK ABOUT HER SISTER.

Two more minutes in the segment. *All right, fine. I'll do it your way.* I waited for my guest to finish answering my previous question and then I asked softly, "And how did your sister feel about all of this?"

She looked at me stunned. It was like I'd just loudly farted in church.

"My sister, Tom, is dead."

Oh boy. *And join us for tonight's Megabucks drawing when the jackpot will be a kazillion dollars.*

Ricky Gervais was years away from creating the awkward character of David Brent for the original British version of *The Office,* but my slithery recovery could well have been inspirational had he been watching Boston television that afternoon.

"Yes, I know that," I lied, my brow now dotted with sweat, "but had she *lived* how do you think she'd have felt?"

Smooth, eh?

Fortunately I was more on my game when former president Jimmy Carter was my guest. I'd interviewed him once before, in 1988, when he came to Boston to promote his book *An Outdoor Journal,* a chronicle of his childhood fishing and hunting adventures. This second time, in January of 1993, he was promoting another book, *Turning Point,* about election fraud in Georgia in 1962. On both occasions I was struck by how present he seemed, his eye contact direct and his handshake firm. We had an easy rapport, due largely to how at ease he made everyone around him feel.

A few days before the show I'd read a newspaper poll about Americans' attitudes toward their former presidents. Jimmy Carter topped the list of most highly regarded after leaving office. The man who had denied him a second term, Ronald Reagan, lagged behind, still smarting from the criticism he'd received after traveling to Japan in 1989 and collecting two million dollars for giving two speeches. Carter, by contrast, spent part of his time post–Pennsylvania Avenue helping to build houses with Habitat for Humanity (for free).

With that story in mind, I decided to take a time-out from discussing historic elections and turn to some more recent returns.

"Given that Americans hold you in higher regard than the man who beat you," I said after citing the poll results, "there has to be a part of you that just says, 'Yes!'" And I pumped my fist for emphasis.

I waited a beat for a diplomatic, evasive, politician's answer. Instead, with a twinkle in his eye, he pumped *his* fist and said, "*Yes!*"

The studio audience, which for this broadcast required quite a few extra chairs, exploded in laughter and applause. Carter's reaction was genuine and endearing, and along with Marie Osmond's "Oh, crap!" it ranks among my favorite career memories.

Would I have asked the question if earlier he'd seemed distracted or impatient? Maybe, but most probably not. But because he felt totally present and relaxed, I relaxed, too. That enabled me to relate to him not just as a former leader of the free world, but also as a guy who might feel pretty good about besting his old rival at something.

That moment, of all the moments from all the shows over my six years as *People Are Talking* host, would, about a year later, be my ticket to national television. Peter Faiman, known for directing the movie *Crocodile Dundee* and, in his native Australia, for smoothly directing massive live television events, had been hired by Rupert Murdoch to develop the live programming for a new cable network, fX. While wading through piles of tapes submitted by agents hoping to land jobs for their clients, he saw Jimmy Carter pump his fist and say, *"Yes!"* As a result, my agent got a call. From that call I got an audition, which led to a job, which led to everything that's happened since.

So, in a way, I have Jimmy Carter to thank for *Dancing with the Stars.*

But I'm getting ahead of myself. What's more, I could just as easily pull on a *different* strand in my life's tapestry and find that one just as responsible for my career today. (*The interconnectedness of all things is a central pillar of Zen, Grasshopper.*) So, leaving Jimmy Carter's contribution aside for the moment, here's another reason, to paraphrase Popeye, I am where I am.

I was downsized.

14

LASSIE'S CHOICE

SOMETIMES YOU HAVE TO DROWN A FEW PUPPIES."

By 1993, local television in Boston had lost much of its local flavor. Public-service programming, original documentaries, and almost anything else outside a station's news department had fallen prey to media consolidation, deregulation, and the exalted bottom line. My wife, Lois, who became a producer with the WBZ documentary unit after we left New Hampshire, had seen the writing on the wall years earlier and resigned in dismay. I think the final straw for her was when the documentary unit produced "Ice Cream Wars," a poorly disguised infomercial for a number of the station's sweeter sponsors shot at Boston's Faneuil Hall and promoted as a consumer taste test.

Guess who was the host. You got it. Her husband.

On *America's Funniest Home Videos* we often do shows that promote Disney, our parent company. We show up in Disney World or on a Disney cruise ship, or we invite Mickey and the gang to join me on the *AFV* set. Given that I'm an arrested adolescent and was a fan of the Mouse House well before being on the payroll, I look forward to them each season. Those shows are *also* glorified infomercials, but, unlike "Ice Cream Wars" and the documentary unit, they're not produced by ABC News.

WBZ-TV management scheduled an employee retreat to help us understand the new economic realities of the industry and to welcome us aboard this bandwagon of change. Welcome *some* of us aboard, anyway. The ones who didn't drown.

During one of the seminars, we were told the story of the dog and her puppies. I don't remember it exactly, but, with some poetic license, here's the gist. I call the corporate consultant's tale *Lassie's Choice.*

Once upon a time a dog and her puppies were crossing a raging river. They were on a long journey and had weathered many challenges. But now the dog knew she no longer had the strength or milk to feed all her puppies. She had two choices. She could divide her limited resources among all the puppies and none would have enough to survive. Or, she could drown a few and feed the rest.

We looked askance at each other after he was finished. From the back of the room someone yipped (like a puppy). Nice bandwagon. Bring a floatie.

It was in this environment that *People Are Talking* was soon reduced from an hour to a half hour. By June of 1993, the show finally ran out of milk. And I ran out of jobs.

My contract with WBZ Radio had already ended in December of '92. The station had morphed into an all-news operation during my time there. While I could see the wisdom of such a move from a market-positioning standpoint (there was no other all-news station in Boston), it left no room for my style of personality-driven show.

The spring of 1993 found Lois and me at a crossroads. Our girls were two and four years old. Because my salary at the time had given us the option, Lois had put her career on hold to be a full-time mom. Now I was about to have the pause button pressed on my career, too. It's great for kids to grow up with two parents in the home, but at least one of them should have a job.

Then, on the eve of collecting my final *People Are Talking* paycheck, and with no other offers on the horizon, WBZ-TV offered me a job paying six figures to become the anchor of their early-morning news.

I turned it down.

That's right. The same guy who, fourteen years earlier, was flat broke, freezing, and staring down a floating pig fetus said no thanks.

And that brings us to, as Jon Stewart would say, our "moment of Zen."

Striving to live in the present moment doesn't mean you shouldn't plan for the future. Quite the contrary. In my experience, being fully present and alive in the *now* makes you better able to see the possible *then*s. All things in life are transitory, even life itself, but *especially* TV shows. Most of them, if you're lucky, have the life span of a hummingbird. Every show that has ever been on television eventually has gone or will go away. There will someday be a last dance on *Dancing with the Stars* and a final crotch hit (reruns excepted) on *America's Funniest Home Videos*. Because I know that *now*, I plan for it. I save. I write a book. I keep a good relationship with our daughters so they'll choose a nice rest home for me. *(Someplace with a spa, girls, OK?)*

It's not fatalism. It's realism. And embracing that knowledge keeps me focused on the present, which helps me plan for the future. Think of it as a motivational Möbius strip.

Hi, I'm Tom, your Zen financial planner. Let's go to our first call. You're on the air.

Hi, Tom. I have a question about, um, hi, *Tom?*

Could you turn your radio down?

I don't have a radio. I'm having this conversation with myself.

Right. Then turn down the other voices in our head.

Will do. Sorry. Anyway, I said no to a job offer because I felt it would take me down the wrong career path. Have I made a mistake?

Who is to say what is a mistake and what is wisdom?

You're not answering my question.

I'm a Zen financial planner. That's how we do things.

Oh.

Did you save any money for a rainy day?

Yes. We have a few months' breathing room.

Good. Breath is the fuel of meditation. Rain brings nourishment.

But we have two young children.

Better to water new flowers with hope than with regret.

Thanks, Riddler. Could you give me something a little less vague?

Buy low, sell high. That's a favorite. Oh, have I told you the one about the sound of one hand clapping? The tree falling in the forest?

Right. Is there anyone else I can talk to?

Sorry, we have to take a break. The Zen financial planner will be back after this word from our sponsor, Karma Cleaners, the place to go "When Your Chakra Needs to Shine."

I've always loved the story of Sylvester Stallone refusing to sell his script for the first *Rocky* unless he could star in it. He was flat broke. A major studio was dangling a fat, green carrot in front of him if he'd just let them buy it as a starring vehicle for someone else. He held firm. That's what Adrian—I mean *Lois*—and I decided to do, too.

What happened next was Magic.

15

HOWDY DOODY,
BYE-BYE BOSTON

D ESPITE THE REPEATED DELAYS, HOWDY DOODY'S SMILE NEVER budged. Buffalo Bob Smith's mood, however, was growing more impatient. I shared Buffalo Bob's sentiments as we sat in the darkened area of the news set and watched our allotted interview time tick away.

A breaking news story had thrown the WBZ-TV *Noon News Hour*'s format out the window. As anchor John Henning talked with the correspondent on the scene, Buffalo Bob and I exchanged frustrated looks.

With *People Are Talking* now gone and my having declined the offer to anchor their morning news, WBZ had come back to me with another offer. This one I accepted: I would do interview segments in the news hour that had absorbed the time period of the talk show. The pay, around half of my old salary, was enough to keep us from dipping into savings as long as we kept to our budget.

Cash-flow issues aside, the new schedule definitely gave me more quality time with Lois and the girls. Preparing each evening for the two four-minute interview slots given to me wasn't terribly taxing. And I truly enjoyed the parade of guests, particularly on this day. After all, I was sitting with one of the biggest stars from the early days of television. Sorry, *two* of the biggest stars.

The posable Howdy on Buffalo Bob's lap was not the marionette featured on *The Howdy Doody Show* in the fifties. *This* Doody, identical in all respects except for the lack of strings, was the one used by Buffalo Bob for personal appearances at conventions. The doll's right arm was raised in a welcoming wave, and the left arm was at its side.

I'd met Buffalo Bob several times during the *4 Today* and *People Are Talking* years and loved having him as a guest. Off camera, he had the bluest sense of humor this side of Florence Henderson and the *Lawrence Welk Show* cast. (I'm not kidding. Mom Brady and some of the Champagne Music Makers could make Sarah Silverman blush.) On camera he retained the infectious energy of his superstar kid-show hosting years.

But we were off camera. Only by five feet, but still off camera.

As John Henning threw to *another* correspondent for an update, Buffalo Bob looked at me, rolled his eyes, and began rapidly moving Howdy Doody's right arm up and down.

I was watching Buffalo Bob Smith jerk off Howdy Doody.

Everyone, sing along: "There's no business like show business!"

Before I could get too comfortable with my new sleeping in and hardly working lifestyle, I received a call from the management of Boston's soft rock station, Magic 106.7. They wanted to know if, in light of my stalled television career (although they were far too nice to say that), I'd consider returning to morning radio. *Are you kidding? Would I consider returning to what is still in many ways my first love? On a station that would encourage me to be as playful as I liked?* I told them, "Possibly."

Lois and I were wined and dined at the Four Seasons Hotel in Boston and drove home that night flattered by the attention and impressed with the people. They made it an easy call. I would soon be Magic's morning man.

As negotiations commenced, a little voice in my head (OK, *one* of the little voices) cautioned me against signing for more than a year.

That hesitation, along with a magnanimous gesture by Magic's GM, Peter Smyth, would prove pivotal even before the year was up.

While there were undoubtedly many—friends and strangers alike—who saw my limited television exposure and return to radio as setbacks, I turned my attention to the half-filled glass. The truth is, once I settled in as Magic's morning man, I felt like I was back in my own skin again. The years as *People Are Talking* host had been great, but I always felt just like that nickname I'd given myself, "Donahue Jr."— like I was playing the *role* of a talk-show host. There were certainly times when I felt completely centered and myself, the Jimmy Carter story being an example, but more often I'd feel, as Tony used to say when critiquing us in South Paris, "off the deck," slightly disconnected from the proceedings. Interestingly, the noon-news interview segments, where I was hired specifically to counterbalance the dryness of the news, made for a better fit. But the time at Magic, surrounded by a welcoming and creative crew, was a godsend. Not since my time in Portsmouth at WHEB had I felt so creatively charged.

About seven months into my one-year contract, in an interesting echo of the calls I'd received while in Portsmouth to audition for TV shows in Boston, my agent's phone began ringing. This time the calls were offers to audition in New York for two new cable networks. One was called America's Talking, fronted by Roger Ailes, who later would launch the Fox News Channel. America's Talking, originating from studios in Fort Lee, New Jersey, would feature—no surprise here—talking Americans, at least several of whom would host their own show. The other was Rupert Murdoch's fX network. It would feature live programming, including a morning show costarring a puppet, originating from a sixty-five-hundred-square-foot loft apartment set in New York's Flatiron District.

I was offered jobs by both networks. That was the good news. But I was still under contract to Magic (the WBZ contract, essentially a freelance agreement, wasn't a problem), and Lois and I had just received a counteroffer to our bid on a great house in Lexington, Massachusetts. Life was good in Boston. But suddenly we were being offered a tantalizing chance to walk in an unexpected direction.

Lois and I lay in bed staring at our bedroom ceiling as if the answer would materialize there like the image of the Virgin Mary appearing on a tortilla.

"I just keep thinking that if we don't do this," I said, "it'll be a constant regret dripping like a leaky faucet for the rest of our lives. We'll always wonder, 'What if?'"

"We could treat it as a one-year experiment," Lois said. "If it doesn't work out, we come back. It's not like we're burning any bridges. The girls will be fine as long as we are."

I thought about the conversation I'd need to have with Peter Smyth at Magic, the one about letting me out of my contract. That *could,* even if it went well, leave a pretty creaky bridge behind.

"OK, we'll do it for a year," I agreed. But first I had to see if I legally could.

Peter Smyth had said during the contract negotiations that he wouldn't stand in my way if "my ship ever came in." I'd told him I'd been tinkering with a sitcom script and had fantasies of it being optioned in Hollywood. That was the only potential ship on the horizon at the time, and it mostly existed only in my head. But now I was going to him with news of two actual national-television opportunities.

"I said I wouldn't stand in the way of your ship," he said. "I wasn't expecting a whole damn fleet."

But, true to his word, and in the face of some heat from *his* bosses up the corporate ladder, he let me out of the contract to take one of the national jobs. Whenever I see him, he never fails to remind me that I owe him. And I never fail to agree with him.

A few times since then, when we've been back in Boston, we've driven past that house we almost bought in Lexington. I'm not sure why, really. Maybe it's to see if another version of us is living there and to see how they're doing. Happily, we always drive there over sturdy bridges.

As for the competing job offers, it ultimately wasn't hard to decide which show to take. Buffalo Bob Smith certainly would have understood. I took the one with the puppet. Which was ironic because, just before the audition, I almost took a hike.

16

READY FOR BREAKFAST

NEW YORK, NEW YORK. THE CITY SO NICE THEY NAMED IT twice."

Whoever "they" were, they obviously hadn't visited *this* neighborhood.

I looked out the window of the unimpressive Eleventh Avenue studio. It was a cold, gray day. Several homeless men in an adjacent park were warming their hands over a trash-can fire. *"New York, New York" indeed. This* part of the city you could have named *once.* I was there to audition for the host position on the planned fX cable morning show and to meet the Australian producer Peter Faiman. I was also counting the minutes until a shuttle flight took me back home to Boston.

Returning to the waiting area, I sat against the far wall and watched silently as several other candidates, including Gary Kroeger, a former cast member of *Saturday Night Live* (the Donnie to Julia Louis-Dreyfus's Marie in the "Blue Christmas" sketch where the Osmond sibs make out with each other), vented nervous energy. Mostly they did this by performing for, and trying to top, each other. It was exhausting. *Why leave all their energy in here?* I thought. By the time they actually auditioned, they'll be spent.

I closed my eyes and began to meditate. Not to calm my nerves. I'd already categorically decided I *would not* work in New York, so I was the picture of contentment, as cool as a cucumber. I meditated to avoid being drawn into the Anxiety Olympics across the room.

"Tom Bergeron?"

I heard my name and opened my eyes. Someone had emerged from the audition room and was scanning for the next victim. "That's me," I said and followed her back in. I was sure this wouldn't take long. I'd just be polite, go through the motions, and hail a cab back to LaGuardia. By evening I'd be home telling Lois about my truly lousy day.

I'd agreed to audition because, one, I was flattered to be asked, and, two, these nice fX people were paying for a round-trip ticket and I wanted to surprise some friends in New York. The friends, who were also veterans of the short-lived Amherst Mime Theater, now had a production company based in Brooklyn Heights. I called from midtown Manhattan suggesting we meet for lunch. They were happy to hear from me but unhappy about a looming deadline on one of their projects. I ate alone. Afterward, to aid in digestion, I embarked on what turned into a much longer walk than I'd expected. By the time I got to my destination at the corner of Eleventh Avenue and West Fifty-second Street, I was already cranky. My mood wasn't improved by the fact that, to my suburbanite eyes, the neighborhood looked better suited to holding auditions for *Intervention*.

I walked into the audition room a curmudgeonly, unmovable Bostonian, absolutely certain of my disinterest in the job. I walked out twenty minutes later humming Gershwin and wondering if I could afford to live anywhere near Central Park. The reason for my sudden—*drank the Kool-Aid*—transformation? Peter Faiman. He welcomed me as if we were already old friends. Within seconds we were standing by a cardboard mockup of the New York loft apartment being created to house a varied lineup of live television shows. This would be like televised radio, he said: loose, improvisational, and alive.

"There is nothing like it on American television," he declared with obvious pride. He was right.

There was certainly nothing like it in Fort Lee, New Jersey, where

America's Talking would launch. My meeting there days earlier with Roger Ailes had gone well but left me unimpressed. That network seemed like a disjointed parade of standard-issue talk shows. fX seemed like a mold breaker.

Faced with Peter's sales pitch, my firm disinterest disintegrated. I was officially stoked. And now it was time for the audition itself. All I remember of that, apart from the sensation of being completely "in the zone," was being instructed to riff with a guy wearing an ugly puppet. *Sure,* I thought, *why not? No way will this whole puppet thing make it to air anyway.*

Wrong again, Tom.

As I left the audition room Gary Kroeger, who was still in the waiting area, called over to me.

"I hear it went really well in there."

"Yeah, I guess so," I said, still buzzing from the performance adrenalin.

He smiled generously. "They're already writing folk songs about it."

I laughed.

Months earlier, before "the fleet" sailed in, I'd been talking to a friend at WBZ about something that had begun to nag at me.

"I'm only thirty-eight," I told her, discounting the fact that the phrase "only thirty-eight," from a certain perspective, was like Barney saying he was, "only a dinosaur."

"I'm not ready to plateau," I continued. "I'm not ready to say, 'This is it' for my career."

She listened sympathetically. "Where would you want to go next?"

She'd asked the sixty-four-thousand-dollar question. And I had no answer. In my personal life, with Lois and the girls, I was exactly where I wanted to be. Professionally, in Boston anyway, unless I wanted to reconsider being a TV news anchor, I'd painted myself into a corner. It was a pretty good corner, what with the morning show at

Magic and the interview segments on the midday news, but it was a corner nonetheless.

Then, suddenly, after grousing to myself about the long walk and the shabby studio and the homeless guys in the park, the answer to her question became crystal clear. I wanted to go to New York and do *this*. I wanted to be part of the team launching a network whose slogan was "TV Made Fresh Daily." I wanted to work with Peter Faiman, this Australian force of nature who shared my love of improvisation, of live television, and of mining the possibilities of the present moment.

There's a belief epitomized in the bestseller *The Secret* that holds that your thoughts and expectations trigger the "Law of Attraction" and bring to you the things you expect, be they positive or negative. Put another way by Henry Ford, "Whether you think you can or think you can't, you're right."

As a longtime meditator who has already admitted to a glass-half-full philosophy, I'd be hard-pressed to argue against that basic premise. Particularly when it keeps proving itself in my life.

Before hopping in a cab outside the studio on Eleventh Avenue for the ride back to LaGuardia, I stood on the sidewalk, took a deep breath, and paused to appreciate the moment. The neighborhood looked quite different to me now. In fact, the burning trash can in the park seemed downright *quaint*. Mentally, I began painting myself out of that corner and into a whole new wing.

Of course, as with any new construction, there'd be some unexpected costs along the way.

17

AND NOW FOR SOMETHING
COMPLETELY DIFFERENT
(with Apologies to Monty Python)

BREAKFAST TIME DEBUTED JUNE 1, 1994, AS THE FIRST PROGRAM on the first morning of the fX network. Today it's better known as FX (much more *uppercase*) and contains no hint of its live-television birth, but on that late spring morning, with an eager, charismatic cast raring to go, the future of cable television felt like it was ours for the taking. And for me, it was the job of a lifetime, hosting a show that was all live and, apart from a rundown I referred to as "the first draft," all improvised. I still miss it.

While never a ratings juggernaut—more a jugger-*not*—it became, during its almost two-year run, a critical darling, earning rave reviews from *TV Guide, Newsweek, Entertainment Weekly,* the *Los Angeles Times,* and Josh, a blogger on IMDB.com:

> *I have to say, this was the best morning show EVER. Imagine this: a studio that's really a huge apartment in New York City, interviews are done anywhere and everywhere (even the bathroom!), one of the hosts is a puppet named Bob, the weather is not only informative, but hilarious, and speaking of weather, the weather man's face was never seen (he always hid behind a newspaper when they got shots of him in his "booth"). Add some celebrities to interview, some awesome segments from the*

*"Road Warriors," who brought new meaning to the on location
interview, and do some dancing on Friday, and what do you
have? Breakfast Time, the all in one morning show for men and
women of all ages, and especially those who are, let's say -
young at heart. I miss this show SO much, it's not even funny.
This is one show, I would do anything to have on tape. . . . even
if only one episode. I suggest anyone who by any chance has a
tape or knows of someone who has an "episode" on tape,
WATCH it! Cherish it for God's sake! Ok. That's my two cents.*

—Josh

Thank you, Josh. The check's in the mail.

When I'm asked why I think *Dancing with the Stars* became a big
hit, after citing the usual reasons like "sexy costumes" and "teeny,
tiny sexy costumes," I answer, "Chemistry." That's the real glue that
holds that show, or *any* show, together. What holds the costumes together is beyond me.

On *DWTS* you're watching a group of people who genuinely enjoy
one another's company. It's no act. And if it was, if we were only
pretending to be friends, you'd know it. A TV viewer's bullshit meter,
particularly when the viewer is watching *live* television, is an extremely precise instrument.

So it was on *Breakfast Time.* We all just clicked. And the result of
that chemistry, that comfort with each other, was the TV-cast equivalent of a veteran jazz ensemble.

Laurie Hibberd, my cohost, quickly established an eye-rolling
rapport with me and often, while having a sharp sense of humor
herself, provided a stabilizing influence on a crew of Peck's Bad Boys.
A sexy Canadian who'd come to fX by way of hosting an entertainment report on Miami TV called *The Buzz,* Laurie went on post-fX to
report for CBS's *The Early Show.* She also married Regis and Kelly's
(then Regis and Kathie Lee's) producer.

"Melman?" I asked when she hinted about her boyfriend's identity. It was during our getting-acquainted lunch after we'd both been hired.

"No, *Gelman*," she corrected. "Michael Gelman."

"Oh, right. Gelman. Of course."

It became a running joke between us both on and off the air that I kept calling him "Melman" nonetheless. About two years later, for reasons other than name-calling, I'd have my own name placed on a Michael *Gelman* blacklist of sorts. Which is why, despite my repeated appearances everywhere from *The View* to *Oprah,* you've never seen me sitting next to Regis. But that story will have to wait a few pages.

Our announcer/weather man/poet laureate was Jim Kocot, a comedy writer with a gruff voice and a gentle soul whose conceit of hiding behind a copy of *USA Today* whenever he was on camera both added to his mystique and made him quite a few fans at *USA Today.*

Our Road Warriors, two of whom appeared live on location from somewhere in the country each morning, included New Zealander Phil Keoghan, who later would indulge his wanderlust as host of *The Amazing Race.*

Bob the Puppet—or, as I often referred to it, "the wart-laden sock"—was brought to life by the wit, voice, and wrist of Al Rosenberg, a former writer and performer with Howard Stern and Don Imus. In Al's hands, or, more precisely, *on* his hand, Bob emerged as the Fonzie of our Happy Days together, a supporting player who quickly became the symbol of the show. Bob was our Greek chorus, free to comment on the proceedings with wicked humor in a way we humans couldn't. He also became our unlikely sex symbol, smooched by countless actresses (and the occasional actor) to the musical strains of Marcie Blaine's "Bobby's Girl."

The best example of Bob's popularity among both his cast mates and our avid viewers was the day the band the Bottle Rockets appeared on *Breakfast Time.* They'd performed in concert the night before and had parked their tour bus outside the fX studios on Twenty-sixth Street to catch a few hours' sleep before appearing on the show. *During* the show, because we had a fully functional apartment set, viewers watched them trudge wearily into our bathroom to shower, brush their teeth, and get ready to perform. Then, during a commercial break, they informed our producer that "the puppet has to go" or they wouldn't play. Once back from the commercial, I informed the viewers of their ultimatum. We put it to a vote. Should Bob or the Bottle Rockets be sent packing? The fX fax machine and e-mail address soon delivered the landslide verdict.

Bye-bye, Bottle Rockets.

McGovern had fared better against Nixon than they had against Bob the Puppet. As Bob gloated mercilessly, an exterior camera showed the pissed-off band members loading their equipment back into the bus and driving away down Fifth Avenue.

When good sport Bob Barker showed up to promote his golf-course smackdown cameo in Adam Sandler's movie *Happy Gilmore* (a classic scene, to be sure), we asked if he'd be willing to play "Hard Hat Price Is Right" on our Fifth Avenue sidewalk with the guys repairing a burst water main. He said yes. The improvised game show featured the city workers trying to guess the retail value of their jackhammers and tool belts. Bob, with whom I'd share a Daytime Emmy in 2000 (him for *The Price Is Right,* me for *Hollywood Squares*), was without a doubt the most entertaining sidewalk game-show host New York City had ever seen.

When *NYPD Blue* was shooting a scene on the next block (and within range of our cameras), I strolled past actual New York City police officers hired for security and delivered a bag of doughnuts, in the middle of a scene being filmed, to a startled Dennis Franz and a furious Jimmy Smits. It took Laurie's diplomatic skills and a bit of flirting to restore the peace once I'd scurried back to the apartment.

Mary Tyler Moore's appearance on the show gave me a unique opportunity. With the theme from *The Dick Van Dyke Show* playing overhead, I did a pratfall over an ottoman in our game room, much as Van Dyke had famously done one in the opening credits of their classic sitcom. I asked her to critique it.

"You telegraphed it," she said. "You can't look like you know it's coming." She was absolutely right.

She, later, was so effusive about the furnishings in our loft apartment set that I impulsively offered her a chance to play a variation of *Supermarket Sweep.*

"I'll give you sixty seconds on the clock. Go through the apartment and see what you like. Whatever you can carry you can keep."

Our brilliant audio engineer, Rob Alexander, instantly found the perfect music to accompany Mary's march. By the end of the minute she'd accumulated shoes, artwork, and, if memory serves, even a lamp. The last shot of her appearance that day was her getting into a stretch limo loaded down with goodies and declaring, "I love this show!"

On Thanksgiving, unable to compete with the Macy's parade uptown (and denied a parade permit by the city), we instead had a Thanksgiving Day Street Crossing. This featured a few handmade floats with good sports like Olympian Nancy Kerrigan and Bob "Captain Kangaroo" Keeshan inching across Fifth Avenue whenever we got the walk signal.

That, in a nutshell, was *Breakfast Time.* For me it was like dying and going to improv heaven.

Peter Faiman had moved back to Los Angeles during the first year of *Breakfast Time* to take a job as Twentieth Television's president of production. At first I took his departure hard. Even though he would still be overseeing the show, it would be from three thousand miles away. I'd come to rely on both his creative energy and his friendship. I soon learned, however, that in his new position he, along with *Breakfast Time* fan and Twentieth president Greg Meidel, planned to take the show to the majors, to the Fox Network. Until now, the experience had been like batting four hundred on a Triple A team—*minor league* heaven. Now I could die and go to *heaven* heaven.

At least that was the plan. But where does that road go that's paved with good intentions? Right. To the place where no SPF value will protect you.

I have two problems with writing about *Breakfast Time*. One, I have so many fond memories of the show that I might never get around to writing about *Hollywood Squares, America's Funniest Home Videos,* or *Dancing with the Stars.* Two, writing about *Breakfast Time* means I also have to write about *Fox After Breakfast,* the Fox Network spin-off and ultimate example of "be careful what you wish for."

Here's a suggestion: go to YouTube and type in "fX Breakfast Time." I just did, and there are (as of this writing) twenty-seven videos from the show. They include this link to our favorite celebrity guests: http://www.youtube.com/watch?v=qYiIC-P4F0o. They also include some highlights of our first year: http://www.youtube.com/watch?v=fBT-ywhNKoU&feature=related. Watch some, and let me know what you think at bergeronbook@aol.com.

In the meantime I'll go get the next chapter ready. It'll require lots of aloe and humble pie. Because both literally and figuratively, I'm about to get burned.

18

WHY THE RED FACE?

L AS VEGAS, NEVADA. CAESAR'S PALACE. OUR PRESENTATION TO the Fox affiliates in the massive auditorium was a hit. We (myself, Peter Faiman, and Twentieth VP J. B. Blunck) had put together a pitch tape showing me wandering California's Venice Beach questioning various characters about a possible Fox morning show. The highlight involved me explaining the concept of Bob the Puppet to a guy who looked like he had Martians on speed dial. As the tape played on a large screen I waited in the wings, listening with relief to the laughter and applause from the crowd. As it finished, I walked onstage wearing a sandwich board that read Have Show, Will Host.

It went better than we dared hope. Afterward, there was palpable excitement about taking fX's critical darling *Breakfast Time* and transforming it into the Fox Network's first morning show. Basking in the presentation's afterglow, Lois and I joined Rupert Murdoch's then wife Anna and several others for lunch.

It was there, as my performance adrenaline faded, that I began to feel like I was beginning to glow myself.

"You look flushed," Lois said. "Are you feeling OK?"

"I don't know." I felt my cheek. It was hot to the touch. "I'm starting to feel a little weird."

I'd prepared for the presentation, as I often prepare for big days, by rising early, meditating, and hitting the gym. One impulsive addition to that regimen came when, after my run, I noticed a few tanning

booths in a room off the main workout area. I hadn't been in a tanning booth in around fifteen years, but I thought a touch of faux sunshine might be nice for the occasion. I bought a session and climbed
onto the tanning bed.

Then I fell asleep.

As I later discovered, fifteen years is more than enough time to
develop higher-intensity tanning bulbs. That never crossed my mind.
The way I figured it, if a half hour on the bed was good in 1981, it
was probably fine in 1996. Boy, was I wrong.

I felt fine until lunch, probably because I'd been hyperfocused on
the presentation. Once that was behind me, my behind, among other
places, began to heat up. A lot.

Lois watched the transformation and prepared to spring into action. While I'd been working out in the gym and napping on the tanning bed, she'd been in the salon near the fitness center getting her
hair done. As luck would have it, she'd struck up a conversation with
a woman who gave facials in the salon—and worked with burn victims at the local hospital. My wife had been looking for me to "pop,"
if you will, ever since I interrupted their conversation to tell her what
happened.

We made our apologies and headed straight to our room. By the
time we got there I was in real pain and sweating profusely. And I
looked like a hairy tomato.

"Lie down," she said, now in full Florence Nightingale mode. "I'm
giving you some ibuprofen." Then, as the woman in the salon had
suggested, she proceeded to wet some towels and cover me with them
as I stretched out, sizzling, on the bed. She left me there while, in less
than an hour, she bought out what must have been Las Vegas's entire
supply of aloe gel.

For the next several hours it was slather, rinse, and repeat. She'd
cover me with aloe gel, drape me with wet towels, and then check
my body temperature. Any sign of fever would be the cue to visit the
salon's facial lady—at her other job.

To complicate matters further, an important dinner loomed that evening with Fox's biggest affiliates. While Lois's nursing efforts had saved me from a trip to the hospital, apparently there was no getting out of the dinner.

"But he looks like a cooked lobster," Lois told Peter and J.B. on the phone in a vain attempt to cancel. No dice. Our dinner guests were the top guns of the Fox station group. Their level of support could make or break *Breakfast Time*'s network fortunes. Plus, they'd seen me only hours earlier dazzling them from the stage at Caesar's. It could be costly for me to suddenly be a no-show.

By the time we left the room I was *feeling* somewhat better, having absorbed a truckload of aloe, but I still looked ridiculous. Even Lois's attempt to apply some makeup couldn't disguise my Mr. Tomato Head.

Many Fox stations aired *I Love Lucy* reruns every morning. As a result, these people had seen Ricky Ricardo stare dumbfounded at Lucy countless times. That's pretty much the reaction they gave me when I entered the room.

Once Peter and J.B. got a look at me, they decided it was better to make apologies for my absence than have me stick around frightening the affiliates. Lois and I dined happily off the room-service menu.

Over the next week I peeled in places I never knew *could* peel. Flakes of my DNA floated like dandelion tufts every time I moved. It was gross.

As I look back, my tanning booth mishap was a touch of poetic justice, an odd harbinger of what was to come. Because in the next few months, despite all the optimism after Las Vegas, I'd see everything wonderful about *Breakfast Time* get peeled away, too.

There was once a cocky television host who worked on a very special show. One day his show was selected to move to The Network. Upon hearing the news, his friends came over to offer

their congratulations. "Such good luck," they said enthusiasti-
cally. "You got that right" was all the cocky host replied. A few
months later the show, having been tinkered with excessively in
the transition, made its network debut. "How wonderful," the
friends exclaimed. "Maybe," replied the host, who wasn't feel-
ing so cocky all of a sudden. Within weeks the new network
executives fired the show's cohost and demanded a radical pup-
petectomy. Now Laurie and Bob were gone, and the host was
bewildered and angry. His friends offered their sympathy, say-
ing, "How awful." The host stared into space. "What time does
the bar next door open?" he asked no one in particular. Several
months later, the host stood on the same set where he'd once
been part of a truly wonderful experience. Nothing of that old
magic remained. He decided to quit. "How awful," exclaimed
the bar owner next door. "Not really," replied the host's liver.

What made the implosion of *Fox After Breakfast*—as the network
version was known—particularly hard was the knowledge that I'd
been complicit in the carnage. I'd allowed the fluffing of my ego
(*You're the star of the show, Tom. We'll build it around you*) to blind me
to the real reason the fX version was a hit: the team. It's no coinci-
dence that during this period I'd stopped meditating, stopped listening to the concerned council of those closest to me (especially Lois),
and stopped trusting my own gut instincts.

According to Google and Proverbs 16:18, *"Pride goeth before de-*
struction, and a haughty spirit before a fall."

I'd goeth before too long myself. But not before getting juiced.

19

KILL THE PUPPET

WHEN I SAW YOU JUMP INTO THAT ORANGE JUICE, I KNEW THE show was OK."

That misdiagnosis of *Fox After Breakfast*'s fortunes came from Jim Kocot, one of *Breakfast Time*'s true treasures, and one of the first casualties of the move to the network. He was referring to my decision on that morning's live broadcast to jump into a few hundred gallons of vitamin C encased in a six-foot-tall Tropicana glass on Fifth Avenue.

My cohost for the week, Robin Givens, and I were talking with a pediatrician about the importance of a healthy diet for children. The segment was a typical morning-television journey into the obvious, and it was making my head hurt.

I looked at the pediatrician. His lips seemed to be flapping in slow motion. "Blah, blah, immune system, blah."

I looked at the enormous glass of orange juice. *What would you have done on* Breakfast Time? I thought.

I turned to our other guest, actor Gregory Harrison, who had joined us on the sidewalk. He could give me a ten-finger boost. I looked back at the pediatrician. "Blah, blah, antioxidants, blah."

"Excuse me," I said, cutting him off. "I have to be honest with you. I haven't heard a word you've been saying. I keep looking at that glass of orange juice, and I keep thinking, 'When am I ever going to get a chance like this again?'"

As I turned to Gregory Harrison to ask for help, I began to unclip my microphone from my shirt. In my IFB, the molded plastic earpiece that enables me to hear cues from the control room, Kim Swan, the show's new executive producer (Peter Faiman having been fired by this point), began to yell, "Don't you da—" I yanked the IFB out of my ear.

Placing my heel into Gregory's interlaced hands, I was lifted to the top of the glass and climbed in. Then, holding myself up for dramatic effect, I gave a three-two-one countdown and vanished into the juice. Displaced Tropicana gushed out of the glass and onto Fifth Avenue. I stayed under for a second, savoring the sting of the juice against my closed eyes, and then sprang back up from the bottom of the glass. I surfaced to the sounds of gasps, laughter, and applause from the guests and crew. I felt wonderful. Until after the show, that is.

There were two distinct camps in the after-show meeting. The remaining *Breakfast Time* veterans, like Road Warrior Phil Keoghan and a number of segment producers, thought it was exactly what this neutered network version was missing. The "newbies," chiefly Kim and her coterie, saw it as the type of recklessness that would send viewers scurrying.

Jim, watching from his home in Stamford, Connecticut, believed he'd seen me reclaim the spirit of the fX show and wanted to compliment me on it.

"I think I'm going to quit," I confessed to him. "I was flipping off the network with fruit juice."

Jim, a class act who remained my friend even after losing his job, took no pleasure in this turn of events. "That's too bad," he said. "I really hoped you could make it work."

So had I. Over the previous months my attempts to remain optimistic about the show's chances had become almost delusional. Even my own agent (who had been fielding some interesting inquiries) advised me to get real. I'd been up to my chin in poop still thinking I'd find a pony in the pile. But I'd finally had it.

The decision to replace Jim's distinctive male voice with a more generic, albeit quite professional female voice was typical of our transitional blunders. I say "our" because I had been given the title of co-executive producer of the network show. It's said that power corrupts. In my case it just made me stupid.

One key change that made me happy, at least initially, was the chance to work alongside Peter Faiman once again. As the network show's executive producer, he'd be spending large chunks of time in New York. I imagined we'd fall back into the devil-may-care, damn-the-torpedoes approach that characterized our work on *Breakfast Time.*

Our philosophy on fX had been "Let's rewrite the book. Let's show them live television like they've never seen it before." Now, in the belief we had to cater to an established daytime audience, we stopped stoking that fire and instead poured water on it. We began to play it safe, to second-guess ourselves. The announcer is too different? Replace him. The theme music is too jazzy? Let's go for sappy. The colors in the apartment set look too muted? Let's make it look like a Crayola box puked on it.

And I went along with each decision, muting the concerned voices of my trusted friends and family and ignoring the nagging ache in my own gut.

"You're selling your soul here," they warned me. "You're losing what made the show special."

"No we're not," I countered a little too firmly, maybe to convince myself. "We're turning a two-hour cult-hit cable show into a one-hour mass-audience network show. We can't just do the same thing."

To some extent that was true. We had sixty minutes instead of two hours. As for the rest, I wish we'd done *our* show instead of the muddled mess we ended up with. We may still have ended up canceled, but it wouldn't have left the bitter aftertaste. There's something to be said for failing on your own terms rather than succeeding on someone else's.

The debut of *Fox After Breakfast* was met with a number of quite favorable reviews. Even a pale imitation of *Breakfast Time* and its loose, improvisational style was a marked departure from other, predictable daytime fare. Among the new show's fans were members of the rock group Yes, who reunited on air with a Fifth Avenue sidewalk concert on October 29, 1996. Within weeks, however, storm clouds were gathering. The show's ratings didn't sustain the initial curiosity tune-in and began to lose some steam. Greg Meidel, our early champion, had left Twentieth to take an executive job at Paramount, leaving *Fox After Breakfast* in the care of, let's say, a less enthusiastic regime.

The Fox executives decided that the way to stem the ratings slide was to fire Laurie Hibberd, my cohost since the first day of *Breakfast Time,* and replace her with guest cohosts. I protested, but not with enough force or conviction to change their minds. To be honest, I wasn't even sure what kind of show I was fighting for at that point.

Laurie and I still see each other for lunch occasionally. When we revisit that time, we do it with long-buried hatchets and a side dish of sick humor. The great memories of working together on *Breakfast Time* outweigh the brief bummer of *Fox After Breakfast*. Live and learn. It's her husband, Michael Gelman, who holds the grudge.

And *that's* why you've never seen me on *Live with Regis and Kelly.*

Well, that's part of the reason. From Michael's perspective (as explained to me by Laurie), it wasn't just that I didn't, in his estimation, fight hard enough for his future wife's job. It's that after she was fired I fought *real hard* and real publicly for Bob the Puppet's job. As a loving husband myself, I can imagine how I'd react if I thought someone casually let my wife hang out to dry and then passionately defended a flapping piece of felt.

By the time the Fox executives took aim at Bob and, by extension, his "handler," Al Rosenberg, I was pretty pissed off. And not just because they were telling me to "kill the puppet." I was pissed at myself for letting it get this far.

I haven't really talked much about my temper, apart from passing mentions, since that story way back at the beginning of the book. Remember? The one where I flunked the test for my third-class operator's license and carried on like a petulant nutcase? I was seventeen then. Now I was forty-one. And I'd stopped meditating, which I'd always thought of as my temper's braking system. On the plus side, by now I was much more creative at being a hothead.

Kill the puppet? That was the last straw. I was about to have a live, network-television temper tantrum. And Sir David Frost was going to help.

20

THE PETER PRINCIPLE POX

THE MUSIC, WHICH I REMEMBER AS WAGNER'S "RIDE OF THE Valkyries," blared from Peter Faiman's open office. He had just been fired. And I felt partially responsible. What I thought to have been an ingenious solution to the network's demand to eliminate Bob the Puppet from the show had backfired. Badly.

"He can't just disappear," I'd complained to Rick Jacobson, the late head of Twentieth Television. Rick and I weren't exactly chummy by this point. "There has to be some acknowledgment of the Save Our Bob campaign, some kind of wrap-up that makes sense within the context of the show."

"As long as he's gone. And soon," Rick said.

Our solution? Promote Bob to the fictional position of Executive in Charge of Program Oversight. In essence, turn him into my boss.

We shot Bob, clad in a bland tie and armless suit coat, in Peter Faiman's soon-to-be-former office. Al Rosenberg, despite the knowledge that this would be his character's swan song, turned in a hilarious performance as the now power-mad puppet.

After the "satellite hook-up" with Bob was finished and we'd effectively written him off the show, I commented on air that that was a classic example of the Peter Principle, which holds that in a hierarchy every employee tends to rise to his level of incompetence.

That's when the shit storm started.

Unbeknownst to me, our Farewell to Bob episode was being

watched on a real satellite hook-up by Rick Jacobson and the head of Fox Television, *Peter* Chernin. The moment the phrase "the Peter Principle" came out of my mouth, it was wrongly assumed I was taking direct aim at the big boss.

Not true. Look, I was angry, but I wasn't suicidal.

Years later, over drinks with my friend (and current big boss) Anne Sweeney, I told her my version of that day. Anne had been chairman and CEO of FX Networks and a staunch defender of *Breakfast Time* when its large budget and small ratings should have doomed it. Our reunion at ABC (where she's now president of the Disney-ABC Television Group) was, in light of *Dancing with the Stars'* success, particularly sweet. But she, too, had always thought I'd gone a bit off my nut that day.

"I swear that wasn't the intent," I told her, laughing. "I thought it was a clever way to give the network what they wanted and just get on with it. Peter Chernin, frankly, didn't factor into it *at all*." I'd met the guy only once and liked him. Who knew he'd think any passing Peter reference would be about *him*?

The real irony is that when I *was* being snarky with the network, they didn't get it. As the first antipuppet wave began to crest, threatening my last major link to *Breakfast Time*, I went on the offensive. Appearing as a guest on the Craig Kilborn version of *The Daily Show*, I announced the formation of the Save Our Bob campaign. S.O.B.

Subtle, eh?

Viewers were encouraged to e-mail, snail-mail, and fax their support for our wart-laden sock. Guests like Richard Lewis donned S.O.B. buttons to support the cause. One notable Bob fan, whom I'd later spend considerable time with, was Whoopi Goldberg. She'd warmed to him (and to me, too, thankfully) when she brought James Brown to the show to help promote her movie *The Associate*. But my favorite moment of all was when Sir David Frost, whose historic interviews with disgraced former president Richard Nixon would inspire a

Broadway hit and Ron Howard movie, agreed to interview Bob the Puppet.

To the fading strains of classical music, a brilliantly dry Frost peered down at Bob as intensely as he had at Tricky Dick.

"Do you feel you've been abandoned by the puppet community?" he asked.

"Yes, yes," Bob answered pathetically. "Kermit, Elmo—none of them return my calls."

It was sublime. Futile, ultimately, but sublime.

The weeks between Bob's departure and my own saw me go from angry, to resigned, to depressed. The only bright spots were provided by my guest cohosts. Each week, adapting an approach once used on the old *Mike Douglas Show,* a different female celebrity joined me. Many, like Marlee Matlin and Melissa Gilbert, are still friends.

Gladys Knight, my first guest host after Laurie's departure, was beyond charming. Her perspective on "the business," which she shared generously with this still-reeling host, was medicinal. And, she let me be a Pip for a day. I established such quick chemistry with Linda Gray of *Dallas* fame that Larry Hagman told her he was jealous. When the late Richard Harris appeared as a guest, we called his ex-wife Ann Turkel on the air because he knew she wanted to cohost, too. So the show had its moments, but they grew fewer and farther between. And it didn't have the old team.

By the time I followed Laurie, Bob, and Peter Faiman out the door, I was definitely ready for something new.

What I got was an ambulance ride.

21

SALMON CHANTED EVENING

I WAS FACE DOWN ON THE BED, SUFFOCATING. I COULDN'T MOVE. In the distance I could hear Lois's voice.

"He's not breathing. Tom! *Tom!!*"

With great effort I jerked back my head and sucked in a lungful of air. Still, I felt like my body was encased in pudding.

"What's your name?" "What date is this?" "How many fingers am I holding up?"

The questions were coming at me from different voices. I was aware of more people in the room now. Their faces felt inches away from my own. *The room. I know where I am. I'm in my bedroom in Connecticut. But who are these people? And why do I feel like I've been partying with Timothy Leary?*

Earlier in the day I'd been in New York, not far from the studio where *Fox After Breakfast* originated. I'd had lunch with two friends, the show's co-executive producer Paul Shavelson and coordinating producer Helen Tierney. We were catching—and kvetching—up.

Paul, a wonderfully creative talent and engaging eccentric, had been a major reason why *Breakfast Time* had continued to shine after Peter Faiman's departure during its first year. Helen, who had produced my Magic FM radio show in Boston—and given me the nickname "Jerky"—was my only choice when Peter offered me the chance to bring one person with me to New York. She'd become like family to Lois, the girls, and me. It was mostly her warnings about the Fox show, along with Lois's, that I'd chosen to ignore.

It had been several weeks since I wearily cashed in all my vacation time, effectively quitting *Fox After Breakfast*. Paul had cautioned me that the network wasn't likely to welcome me back from my break. I assured him I wasn't planning on returning anyway. Basically, Fox and I had decided it was best if we saw other people.

Paul picked the restaurant for our bittersweet reunion. I had the salmon. Bad choice, as it turned out. Within hours I'd be a candidate for the Food Poisoning Hall of Fame. Not that Lois and the medical team knew it at the time. They all thought I was having a major heart attack. So, immediately after I'd aced the questions in the paramedics lightning round, we moved right into the "hightail it to the hospital" round.

I can be glib about it now. That night, however, it was frightening. Lois's mom, whom we absolutely adored, had died earlier in the year from cancer. Now my wife thought her husband was dying, too. And the paramedics, who at one point said, "He's going into cardiac arrest," weren't very reassuring. Lucky for me, Lois stopped them from administering an adrenaline shot after they laid me out in the entranceway downstairs.

I'd passed out on the stretcher as they tried to maneuver me down the stairs. I remember, as they moved me along the upstairs hall, seeing the closed doors of my daughters' bedrooms and being thankful they were both sound asleep. Then, for the first time, I wondered if this was what it felt like when you die. That thought, coupled with the jostling of the stretcher and some major nausea, sent me into a swoon worthy of my favorite Osmond.

The next thing I remember: I was looking up at the light fixture near the front door, trying to recall where I'd seen it before. Lois, having ordered the paramedics to put down their needle, yanked hard on both of my ankles and ordered *me* not to die. We all did exactly what she said. It's never a good idea to mess with a determined redhead.

In the emergency room following the ambulance ride, and still in a major fog, I announced to no one in particular that I wanted to sit up.

"If he wants to sit up, sit him up," I heard someone say. Lois told me later it was the ER doctor.

Several hands moved to my shoulders and back, and suddenly I was upright. I belched. Really loud. Lois and the nurse, who were each holding a standard-issue, liver-shaped plastic puke cup, turned to each other in alarm.

"These aren't going to be big enough," Lois said.

On cue, the Mount St. Helens of salmon lunch specials erupted from my bloated gut.

Seconds later, oblivious to the massive cleanup going on around me, I sighed. The fog cleared.

"That's better," I said.

Over the next two days, a number of follow-up tests were conducted, including a coronary angiogram, to confirm that there was no heart "event." In that test, dye was injected through a catheter that had been inserted into an artery in my upper thigh. Almost immediately my earlobes flushed warm. Within minutes the doctor announced that my heart's plumbing was as clear as a baby's. Which for some reason made me crave a cheeseburger.

The culprit, in addition to the foul fish, appeared to have been my vagus nerve. Apparently, as the food poisoning worked its magic, my stomach bloated and compressed the vagus nerve, which effectively slowed down some functions of my sympathetic and parasympathetic system.

Or something like that.

My sister is the medical professional in the family. Once I redecorated the ER, the pressure released and everything rebooted. I was almost as good as new.

Except that I was also, once again, unemployed.

The excellent coronary angiogram results notwithstanding, the previous year had taken a toll. I was already emotionally and physically depleted even before getting bitch-slapped by bad salmon.

The weekend after I was released from the hospital, we took a medicinal family trip back to Portsmouth. It was there that I finally decided, much to my agent's relief, to take her advice and heed the call of the Roone.

Arledge, that is.

VIVA LIZ VARGAS

I WAS IN THE ABC STUDIOS IN TIMES SQUARE, TAKING A BRIEF break from a satellite radio tour I was doing to promote the new season of *Dancing with the Stars*. Satellite tours, whether for radio or television, involve sitting in a room for about three hours while a passing parade of anchors or DJs offer their variations on essentially the same questions. I've always been greeted warmly during these marathons, so I do my best to give each host a fresh spin on my stock answers. Still, if you don't occasionally stretch your legs, you can fresh-spin yourself silly.

As I stood in the hall talking with the radio tour's producer, Elizabeth Vargas, coanchor of ABC News's long-running magazine show *20/20,* appeared from around a corner. She was promoting an upcoming *20/20* segment on *Good Morning America* and was on her way to the studio. We hadn't seen each other—in three dimensions, anyway—in a while. Quick hugs and updates were exchanged, and then we both had to get back to work.

"I've always had a bit of a crush on you," I confessed.

As she continued on, she said, maybe just to be nice, "Me too."

I come by my crush honestly. Elizabeth and I spent a week together that changed my life.

I'll explain that in a minute. (I know. I'm a tease.)

For months prior to leaving *Fox After Breakfast,* even as I became a daily patron of Dewey's Flatiron pub next door to the studio (vodka having replaced meditation during this period), I stubbornly insisted that the ratings-starved show could be saved.

Babette Perry, my agent since the *People Are Talking* years in Boston, certainly had dealt with me in my full-on Taurus moods before. She knew that I could be impossible to reason with once I'd dug in my heels. But this was the first time she'd ever threatened me *physically.*

"If I have to wrestle you on this one, I will," she promised. She had reason to be exasperated.

"They've promised to promote the show during February sweeps," I said. "If they don't come through, I'll meet with him."

Him was the late Roone Arledge, one of the true giants of television. As a biography from the Museum of Broadcast Communications Web site puts it, he "had a more profound impact on the development of television news and sports programming and presentation than any other individual." And he wanted to meet with *me* about joining *Good Morning America.*

I couldn't, I told Babette. I was too busy rallying support for a puppet.

February, one of the year's most important ratings periods, came and went. So did the promise of prime-time promotion for *Fox After Breakfast.* Fox, with only two hours of programming each night, had limited promo space available. Too limited to waste on a struggling morning show. There were other priorities, I was told—shows in prime time that needed the attention more.

"You can call Roone now," I said to my agent.

"Good," she said. "Now I don't have to kill you."

Lunch was scheduled at his favorite Italian restaurant in Manhattan. Beforehand, Babette briefed me on the conversations she'd been having with his office.

"They're making major changes at *Good Morning America.* They've been watching you since *Breakfast Time* and think you're just what the show needs."

I was flattered but puzzled. "Really? And what is *that*, exactly?"

"They want it to be looser, more improvisational. Especially in the second hour."

Good Morning America, Today, and CBS's *The Early Show* all focus on newsmaker interviews in their 7 a.m. hour and shift gears to lifestyle and entertainment topics later. *People Are Talking* had given me plenty of practice covering the whole spectrum. It wasn't uncommon for me to spend one day grilling a guest like rejected Supreme Court nominee Robert Bork and the next day coochie-cooing with Charo.

Interestingly, during my stint in Boston, a competing talk show debuted in 1988 called *Talk of the Town.* The husband of a good friend hosted it: Matt Lauer.

Matt's first wife, Nancy Alspaugh, was the producer of WBZ-TV's *Evening Magazine,* on which I'd occasionally guest-host. Before taking the Boston job, Matt had been host of *P.M. Magazine* in Providence, Rhode Island. (It was called *Evening* on the Westinghouse-owned stations, *P.M.* everywhere else.)

Talk of the Town didn't last long, but through no fault of Matt's. He was then, as he is now, smart, funny, and completely at ease on live television. When the *Boston Herald* asked me to comment on my vanquished competition, I told them it was a shame Matt worked for a station built on an old Indian burial ground. They couldn't keep *anything* on the air back then, but they should have kept him.

Now, in the midst of being courted to come to *Good Morning America* to take on *Today,* I had even more reason to wish Matt's Boston career had continued.

The lunch with Roone and his associate, ABC News vice president Joanna Bistany, was surreal. I had just spent several days cohosting *Fox After Breakfast* with future *Dancing with the Stars* contestant (and, not to bury the lead, Oscar winner) Marlee Matlin. Roone told me that a number of people within ABC News watched those shows and were impressed.

Marlee and I instantly became friends, a fact I didn't admit to on

Dancing until the night she was eliminated. Any concerns Fox executives had about a deaf woman cohosting a talk show evaporated after the first hour. It was pretty funny, however, watching guest L. L. Cool J's puzzled expression as Marlee would sign a question to his left and Jack Jason, Marlee's interpreter, would speak it over my shoulder to his right.

"I don't know where to look." He laughed.

During the lunch, Roone laid out a scenario that echoed Babette's briefing. *Today* had taken a commanding lead in the morning-show wars, and *GMA* was going to undergo a major overhaul. Longtime coanchor Joan Lunden would leave within months, to be replaced by L.A. news anchor Lisa McCree. Charles Gibson, who would later prove to be ABC News's white knight following the death of Peter Jennings, was likely to leave as well. That's where I would come in. Maybe.

I can't overstate how unlikely this turn of events seemed. One minute I'm butting heads with Fox executives over a failing morning show, and the next I'm having clandestine meetings with Roone Arledge and later—in a hotel suite, of all places—with ABC News president David Westin about possibly taking over *Good Morning America*. If Allen Funt had jumped out of the bathroom and told me I was on *Candid Camera*, I wouldn't have been surprised.

It's not that I didn't think I could do it. I was just surprised *they* thought I could do it. Being on ABC News's radar while I was exchanging quips with a puppet was the last thing I expected.

Once I finally left *Fox After Breakfast*, it was decided I'd do a test week on *GMA* while Charles Gibson was on vacation. If it went well, then we'd talk. If not, then we wouldn't. Joan Lunden would be off that week, too. The transition to Lisa McCree was still a little way off.

So, saints be praised, I got to work with Elizabeth Vargas.

On the eve of my test week the phone rang at our house in Connecticut. Lois answered it and called to me.

"Tom, David Hartman is on the phone for you." We exchanged *How cool is this?* expressions as I picked up the extension.

David had been *Good Morning America*'s first host when it debuted in 1975, and he remained there, for most of those years at the top of the ratings heap, until 1987. We'd met when he'd been a guest on *Breakfast Time.* He remembered that appearance fondly, as did I, and, after a mutual friend told him about my audition, he'd called to offer his support.

"I won't wish you luck because you don't need it," he said generously. "Just be yourself. Have fun. I'll be watching."

We chatted a bit, and I thanked him profusely before hanging up. His call felt like the ultimate good-luck charm (although I was still on the lookout for Allen Funt).

The week went beautifully, even earning me a "cheer" in the "Cheers and Jeers" section of *TV Guide.* I owe a lot of that to Elizabeth. She was warm and welcoming and put me completely at ease. Plus, we had great chemistry on air.

Soon after, a contract was negotiated that named me Charlie Gibson's regular fill-in. It also stipulated that by June 1, 1998, barring unforeseen circumstances, I would be announced as the new coanchor of *Good Morning America.*

Cue the unforeseen circumstances.

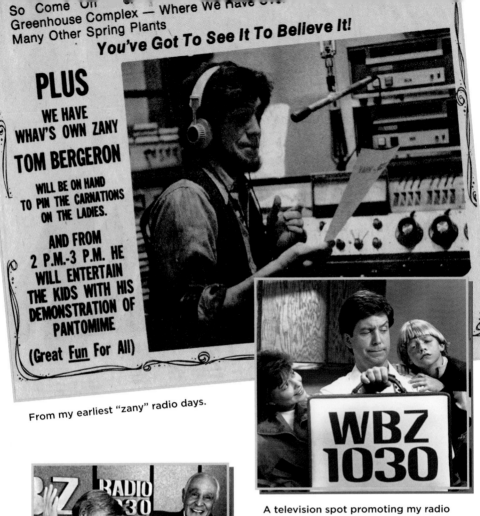

So Come On
Greenhouse Complex — Where We have
Many Other Spring Plants

You've Got To See It To Believe It!

PLUS

WE HAVE
WHAV'S OWN ZANY

TOM BERGERON

WILL BE ON HAND
TO PIN THE CARNATIONS
ON THE LADIES.

AND FROM
2 P.M.-3 P.M. HE
WILL ENTERTAIN
THE KIDS WITH HIS
DEMONSTRATION OF
PANTOMIME

(Great Fun For All)

From my earliest "zany" radio days.

A television spot promoting my radio
show. I am holding the world's largest
promotional lunchbox.

Three generations of WBZ
"Morning Men." (1990)

With Sid Caesar and Imogene Coca
in the WBZ Radio studio.

Tom Bergeron - Radio Personality Explores Silent World Of Mime

By M...

Tom returned to WHAV a...

"Some o...
re-bounding...
Tom Berger...
station anno...
wound up...
through tha...
about the li...

Mime is...
white-faced...
some situa...

Working...
can run the...
like a larg...
But bein...
that easy...
rememberi...
physical...
getting hu...
Stooges f...
radio stat...
he intervi...
on severa...

He reca...
when he...
children,...
learn mo...
was prob...
suddenly...
floor. We...
said Tom...

But a...
Tom wa...
when "a...
Right th...
either le...
or quit,"...

C...
to f...
The...
wh...
and...
opp...

M...
cea...
De...
pos...
An...

wi...
inf...
bu...

pc...
to...
ar...
"I...
h...
M...

The Haverhill Independent

Me during my Marcel Mar-so-so period.

...ere is a sens...
...ence and acto...
...g of his ra...
...norning is m...
...about his 6 a...
...HAV.
...says, is tha...
...nd sound lik...

...share with ot...
...us are people...
...into life," w...
...coming fro...

...ence on stage...
...otions. The sta...
..." he adds.
...isn't always...
...ver since he...
...en intereste...
...falling and...
getting hurt. In fact, he was a real T...
...nd while working for...
...uring his high school y...
...Mo and Larry via the p...
...erent occasions.
...ith much amusement...
...when he was working with an audier...
...d came on sta...
...to mime. The...
...ed, said Tom...
...little puddle o...
...way from the...

...that perform...
...to be an ele...
...I panicked, f...
..."I decided I...
...it what I was...

...as fortunate e...
...e Celebration...
...by Tony Mont...
...done so much...
...eyes to a my...

...d with Marce...
...'s teacher, I...
...Tom, Monta...
...he more gi...

...ery long abou...
...how Montana...
...his concept o...
...of life.
...Maine to exp...
...rt of mime. He...
...to escape performing and investi...
art and share his discoveries, sa...
"He is a giver and he wants you to...
he isn't just trying to create lit...
Montanaro's," he adds.
Tom spent the summer of 197...
Maine theater, very lonely and fri...
but he returned the second sumr...
and found it to be a fantastic exp...

Doing street mime in Montreal in the '70s anticipating the reaction I'd get for cohosting the Emmys in 2008. The Haverhill Gazette

Tom Bergeron. The joy that Bergeron brings to young...

[Larry Kennedy Photo]

Always the snappy dresser, I embark on my 1980 radio series *The Month Across America*.

My 1982 live broadcast and one-man show at Theatre by the Sea in Portsmouth, New Hampshire.

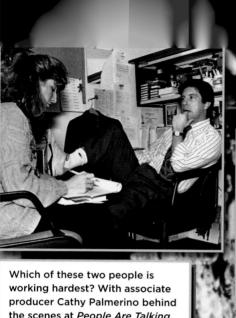

Which of these two people is working hardest? With associate producer Cathy Palmerino behind the scenes at *People Are Talking*.

President Jimmy Carter on the set of Boston's *People Are Talking* in 1993. In a way, he helped me get *Dancing with the Stars*.

Warming up the *People Are Talking* audience. I think that's Marie Osmond fainting in front of me.

Bob

WINNING THE CRITICS OVER WITH ORIGINALITY.

BreakfASt TIME

Tom

Laurie

f/X

GET INVOLVED WITH A WINNER.

BreakfAst TIME

Me with Phil Keoghan (walking behind float) and Nancy Kerrigan on *Breakfast Time*'s low-budget Thanksgiving Day street crossing.

With Timothy Dalton. James Bond and I do spit takes.

On *Fox After Breakfast*, Gladys Knight with three Pips.

Laurie Hibberd, Bob the Puppet, and me with Gillian Anderson on the debut of *Fox After Breakfast*.

In the bedroom with Howard Stern and Robin Quivers.

Frost/Bob

Carol Alt and me having breakfast with Malcolm X's widow, the late Betty Shabazz.

Paula Abdul and me pre-Simon and Bruno.

With Aretha Franklin and Marlee Matlin.

With cohost Marla Maples and her then husband "The Donald," all smiles on a Valentine's Day show.

Bob Saget and I both hit on Phyllis Diller.

After this little stunt,

I didn't catch a cold for three years.

With John Ritter backstage at *Hollywood Squares*. I miss sharing laughs with him.

Establishing a tic-tac-toe-hold.

Henry Winkler and me laughing, possibly about those yellow pants.

Comforting nervous guests is part of a good host's duties.

Tossing souvenirs to the *Hollywood Squares* audience. This is my best side.

With this haircut,
I was 5'11".

Hollywood Squares promotional shoot. Whoopi
and I have difficulty acting our age. (1998)

The Fonz and I coochie-coo with Charro.

Striking a Charlie's Angels
pose with Kate Jackson
backstage at *Hollywood
Squares*.

This is how I looked in the twenty-second century, on *Star Trek: Enterprise*.

What's a hot Vulcan like you doing in a place like this?

Bergeron 'a lot less boring than I expected'

By Aglaia Pikounis
Eagle-Tribune Writer

HAVERHILL — Tom Bergeron skipped the lengthy inspirational messages so many speakers give to graduates across the country this time of year.

Instead, the Haverhill High graduate and television game show host had a simple request yesterday.

"Be good to yourselves," Mr. Bergeron told Haverhill High seniors who graduate Friday.

Mr. Bergeron, a 1973 graduate, was guest speaker at the Class of 1999 Senior Chapel, an annual tradition where juniors are installed as new senior class officers and awards are given to high-achieving students.

In the school's stifling auditorium — as seniors in their brown and gold caps and gowns wiped the perspiration from their foreheads — Mr. Bergeron warned students of the challenges and stresses that await.

"How many of you have heard of

perfect attendance certificates signed by Mo, Larry and Curly.

"These are a few things you left behind," Mr. Madson said.

Mr. Madson also gave Mr. Bergeron a mock Emmy and original 1974 artwork from the Archie comic strip. Much of the strip is based at the old Haverhill High.

Ken Yuzskus/Eagle-Tribune
Haverhill High graduate and television celebrity Tom Bergeron talks to students at the school yesterday.

ceremonies.

After the Haverhill High Chorus and saxophonists entertained the

longer than my speech," Mr. Bergeron yelled out from his seat.

"It was a lot less boring than I expected," said senior Jennifer R.

Vallieres of Haverhill.

Senior class President Derek W. Griffin, 18, said the event was the last time the class would meet together at school.

"It meant a lot to me," said Derek, son of Susan and Wayne Griffin of Haverhill, "especially since I had to pass on the peace pipe." He was referring to the colorful senior symbol given to the incoming senior class president.

"All the preparation gets you psy-

HAVERHILL HIGH GRADUATION

When: Tomorrow, 6 p.m.

One of my favorite headlines ever.
The Eagle-Tribune

ched for graduation," said Da M. Canfield, 18, daughter of D and Daniel Canfield of Have She plans to study accountin business marketing next ye Northern Essex Community C

"The years just flew by. I believe it's here," she said. "I you know. I went through th book yesterday and started to

Promotional shot for *America's Funniest Home Videos.* I'm cringing at a compromised crotch.

Onstage at "The Annuity," *America's Funniest Home Videos.* The slapstick buffet is the gift that keeps on giving. *Photos by Kevin Harkins, courtesy of* Merrimack Valley Magazine

Heidi Klum and me at
the 2008 Emmys.
(This is drama.)

(This is comedy.)

After the Victoria's
Secret fashion show,
Heidi e-mailed me
that she was ready to
be dropped again.

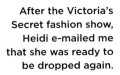

Busting a dance move during a commercial break. © *Adam Larkey/ABC, Inc.*

This is how Marie Osmond looked on *DWTS* when she was conscious. © *Carol Kaelson/ABC, Inc.*

With Cloris—perhaps the funniest lady to grace the *DWTS* stage. © *Kelsey McNeal/ABC, Inc.*

Jason Taylor and me with Captain Kirk's favorite dancer. © *Kelsey McNeal/ABC, Inc.*

Lois.

The day after our daughter Jessica was born, I was already getting frisky.

Our first night out as new parents, in 1988.

One of the hundreds of cartoons I've
drawn for my daughters.

The proud papa with Jessica, age three,
and Samantha, age one.

23

LIVE MCCREE OR DIE

HERE IS A SMALL GOLD PLAQUE ON THE FRONT OF MY DESK AT our vacation home in New Hampshire. It reads, *"McCree Manor, established May 1999. From Cold Shoulder to Warm Hearth."* Here's how it got there.

"How was it?" Lois asked me about the lunch meeting in New York.

It was supposed to be just a casual, low-pressure, getting-to-know-you afternoon for me, Roone Arledge, the *Good Morning America* producer, and Lisa McCree. That's not exactly how it turned out.

"She never looked at me," I answered.

"You're kidding."

"No, I'm not. It was like she was wearing an invisible neck brace. I almost started making faces just to get a reaction."

By this point, the ink on my contract was dry, Joan Lunden had left the show, and Lisa, Our Lady of No Peripheral Vision, had assumed the role of coanchor. I would find out later she'd also assumed the role of Charles Gibson's defender.

In 2000, after I'd won a Daytime Emmy for hosting *Hollywood Squares,* I was interviewed by *People* magazine. They wanted to know what had happened with me and *Good Morning America*.

"To say Lisa and I were chemistry-impaired would be charitable," I told them. "If you were sitting close enough to your television, it actually gave off a wind chill."

Then they contacted Lisa. "Regrettably, he's probably right," she admitted. "I didn't extend myself because of my allegiance to Charlie. I was upset at management trying to nudge him out."

With the benefit of hindsight, I can certainly see her point. I had just come from an experience on *Fox After Breakfast* where I'd been in a wrestling match with management about the show's direction. I can hardly begrudge Lisa the same fight over the direction of *GMA*. Plus, given my penchant for going off script, I probably scared her a little. At the time, however, I wasn't so philosophical, and she was driving me nuts.

The few, awkward weeks I spent on the air with Lisa stood in marked contrast to the breezy few days with Elizabeth Vargas. I was actually worried that *TV Guide* would ask for their "cheer" back. But by then, they'd probably switched to *Today*.

Other than the chemistry issue, there were two reasons I got a house in New Hampshire instead of an anchor role on *Good Morning America*. One reason was that my contract had a penalty clause. As long as I fulfilled my end of the deal, they had to give me the job or cut me a check. The second reason was that Princess Diana died.

By that time, having already read the John Hancock–sized handwriting on the wall, I'd agreed to waive the clause in my contract stating I was to be Charlie's sole fill-in. As a result it was Kevin Newman, *Good Morning America*'s newsreader, who was at the helm when the paparazzi hounded the Princess of Wales to her fatal crash.

Kevin, whose time in Canadian television left him well versed in all things Royal Family, did a wonderful job during some very sad days. Add to that the fact that Lisa would actually make eye contact with him, and my days on the *GMA* fast track were over.

Knowing what I did about the penalty clause, I took it all in stride. But I must admit I was a little rattled when I read the bold headline of the *New York Post*'s entertainment section a few weeks later.

GMA TO TOM: YOU'RE OUT!

Who says there's no such thing as bad publicity?

So Kevin got the job, Lois and I got a house, and, eight months after the new *Good Morning America* team was in place, they were gone, victims of declining ratings. In *their* place? The lovely Diane Sawyer, and that Lazarus of network news, the current number one evening news anchor, Charles Gibson.

And guess who shows up now and again as a special correspondent for *Good Morning America*? That's right, yours truly. And not only does Diane Sawyer look at me, sometimes (with apologies to Lois and Mike Nichols), we also *flirt* a little.

With my eviction notice *New York Post*–ed, it was common knowledge that I was once again a Host for Hire. Sean Perry, now a partner at the Endeavor talent agency, was then an executive with King World productions. He called my agent. We'd had a conversation about a job possibility months earlier, just before I'd signed the *Good Morning America* contract. He understood when I told him I'd be going with them.

"If it doesn't work out," he'd said, probably while gazing into a crystal ball, "maybe we'll talk again."

And we did. My résumé, which was looking more and more like the patchwork glue job of a hostage note, was about to add another square.

Actually, nine of them.

24

WHOOPI'S CUSHION

S O HOW IS BOB?" WHOOPI GOLDBERG ASKED ME AS WE WALKED toward the audition room.

"At my house on a shelf," I answered. "One of them is, anyway." (Two identical Bobs had been made to insure against felt failure.) "Al Rosenberg has the other one."

Whoopi had really enjoyed Bob, the loft-apartment set, and the improvisational feel of *Fox After Breakfast.* She'd been one of our early guests, and certainly our most famous, during that brief period when we were still basking in the glow of favorable reviews and passable ratings.

She was there to promote her movie *The Associate,* and she'd brought along her very game costar Tim Daly and the incomparable James Brown.

The hour flew by. The show's outline was largely abandoned in favor of improvised moments such as a dance-off in our ballroom (yes, our set had a ballroom) between Tim and the Godfather of Soul.

We didn't need Bruno Tonioli to figure out who won *that* one.

In the unsettling months that followed, I'd often look back on Whoopi's visit as a shining example of what the show *should* have been.

While I patiently waited for my penalty-clause check from *Good Morning America,* the story broke that Whoopi had signed to be the center square in King World's revival of *Hollywood Squares*. The hosting job on *Squares* is what Sean Perry and I had talked about pre-*GMA*. When I read they'd signed Whoopi, and after another day of no eye contact from Lisa McCree, I was feeling a bit wistful.

Still, when I was actually available and Sean's second call came, I was back to being stubborn Tom.

"They'd like you to fly to L.A. and audition with Whoopi," Babette told me when she called.

"I don't know," I said. "A game show?"

There was just a beat of silence on the line. Just long enough for Babette to fantasize about beating *me*.

"Listen. This is Roger and Michael King's top priority. They've signed Whoopi Goldberg. They've already got major station clearances. This is a sure thing. Look at Pat Sajak. If you get this you could be set for life."

Now *I* paused. I still wasn't ready to embrace the idea. "It'd be nice to see Whoopi again," I said.

"Right," she said. "Nice to see Whoopi. Whatever. You're the only client I have to arm-twist to take great jobs."

"We've done OK so far," I said.

"You're unemployed."

"OK, except for that."

The audition didn't feel like an audition. Whoopi and I fell right back into the improvisational vibe of her *Fox After Breakfast* appearance. We were like two troublemakers disrupting a class while cracking each other up. John Moffat, one of the show's executive producers, told me later that I got the job in part because I wasn't intimidated by Whoopi.

Intimidated by her? Hardly. Despite the fact we'd met only once before, she felt like an old friend.

As with the *Breakfast Time* audition four years earlier, I returned home with my ambivalence shaken. I'd really enjoyed myself.

My agent called several days later with the verdict. They were offering me the job. King World's only condition was that we'd have to move to Los Angeles.

I turned it down.

OK, not really. Not like I turned down the morning anchor position in Boston during my *last* period of unemployment. What I did was gamble that they, much like Paul Lynde on the original *Hollywood Squares*, were bluffing.

It was an educated gamble. Pat Sajak had been a guest of mine years earlier on *People Are Talking*. I'd asked him what his favorite part of the job was.

He smiled. "You show up in jeans, and there's a suit hanging in your dressing room. You put it on, host the show, go back to your dressing room, and there's another suit. You do this a few more times and you've got a week's worth of shows. Then you go home."

I imagined they'd do much the same with *Hollywood Squares*. Syndicated shows typically produce around 180 shows in a season. That works out to thirty-six weeks of original shows. Assuming they'd shoot five shows a day (which turned out to be the case), you're looking at a whopping thirty-six days of work. Just over a month a year. And for this I had to uproot Lois and the girls? No thank you.

Babette told them my decision. Within hours, Michael King, an extremely persuasive guy, was on the phone. Acting as a one-man Los Angeles Chamber of Commerce, he made the case for us to make the move.

"You'll love it out here," he promised. "The kids will love it. We'll get you into the country club."

There was no way for Michael to know it, and his full-court press was flattering, but trying to woo me with a country-club membership was like trying to woo the Dalai Lama with a juicy steak. I don't golf, and frankly, I'm too much of a loner to want to pay dues to socialize. I held firm.

The next day Babette called. "You win. They've agreed to fly you in for tapings. You don't have to move."

With the main sticking point resolved, the rest of the negotiations proceeded smoothly. And so I prepared for a bicoastal existence that continues to this day. We'd live in Connecticut and I'd work in California. We wouldn't have to move.

That turned out to be somewhat ironic because, a few days before the first taping of *Hollywood Squares,* I *couldn't* move.

25

THE ADVENTURES OF
CAPTAIN SPASM

MY FRIEND CARL REINER (WHOM I MET WHEN HE WAS A GUEST on *People Are Talking*) has a great line that Steve Martin used in his film *L.A. Story.* I agree with it.

"I could never be a woman. I'd stay at home all day playing with my breasts."

Well, maybe not *all* day. But I've got another reason I could never be a woman. Labor pain. Epidural or no epidural, by the time that water breaks you're looking at a heap of hurt. And when it comes to pain, I'm pathetic.

It was a beautiful early evening in the summer of 1998. I was at a neighborhood playground with my daughters, who were now seven and nine years old. We were having some daddy-daughter quality time. Lois was back home visiting with our next-door neighbors. The girls were whizzing by me as I spun them on the small merry-go-round. As I did, another little girl walked toward it with a hopeful look.

"Would you like to get on, too?" I asked.

She nodded.

Here's where common sense is a wonderful thing. Had I *applied* some, I would have waited for the merry-go-round to decelerate and then helped her onto it. Instead, in direct violation of Newton's Third

Law of Motion (*For every action there is an equal and opposite reaction*), I reached out and attempted to stop it cold. All of the force of the no-longer-spinning merry-go-round transferred itself suddenly into my lower back. As it did, something down there snapped like a bad guitar string. My knees buckled. Daddy-daughter quality time had officially ended.

Moving gingerly, I cajoled the girls to the car and carefully drove back home. Once there, while I applied ice to my lower back, Lois, our neighbors, and I all had a good laugh at my expense. *How dumb was that, eh?* It appeared I would survive. I was sore and felt like an idiot, but I was moving.

That night, as I remember it, I slept fine. I'm a little vague because of the seared nova burst of memory that hit as I woke up. Lois had let me sleep in and had taken the girls off to school. I awoke to a bright and beautiful morning. I shifted slightly under the covers, and as I did, not to overstate it or anything, my lower back was gutted by Satan's flaming sword. It was my first-ever massive back spasm.

I believe my exact quote was

"FFFFUUUCCKKK!!!!!!"

Thus began several days of me being scared shitless and whimpering like a baby. I had never experienced anything like that level of pain before. I'd have gladly downed another plate of bad fish if it would have made it stop. As a result I became *very* tense—which, I now know, creates the perfect setting for *another* back spasm.

My doctor arrived a few hours after the inaugural spasm to find me lying bug-eyed on the bedroom floor. Lois, once again patiently playing Florence Nightingale, updated him on the situation.

He nodded thoughtfully and looked down at me. I could see straight up his nostrils. "You probably just pulled something," he said.

Ya think??

Muscle relaxants were prescribed, and I was advised to call if it got worse. *Got* worse*? If it gets worse, get me a gun!*

Good evening and welcome to "The Zen Doctor." Our subject tonight is the mind-body connection. Let's go to our first caller. Hello, you're on the air.

Oww. Damn it.

You're on the air.

I know, I know. Jesus, give me a second. I almost sneezed there and I'm a little tense.

Of course. Back problems?

How did you know?

Lucky guess. What's your question?

I've had an MRI that shows my discs are fine and there's no muscle damage. Still, about twice a year my back seizes up and it scares the hell out of me. What can I take to make it go away?

How about a nice reality check?

Excuse me?

Are there any unresolved issues in your life?

I didn't call to talk about my life. I called to talk about my back.

That's what we are doing.

What's "what we *are* doing"? Are we talking about my back or my life?

Yes.

We're going in circles here.

I'm a Zen Doctor, that's . . .

". . . *how we do things.*" Got it.

Back about a hundred pages ago I told you that I learned two important things during my first stint in radio. *One, the person you should be when you open that microphone is* yourself. *Two, just because you know that first thing doesn't mean you can do it.* It turns out that that's true about more than just hosting a radio show.

For twenty-five years I'd been meditating. I knew about the mind-body connection, both intellectually *and* intuitively. By 1975 Dr. Herbert Benson from Harvard Medical School had published *The Relaxation Response,* a book that offered scientific proof of it. But do you think I even *considered* an emotional trigger to my spasms? Even after the MRI showed that everything was perfectly fine in there?

No, I didn't. I spent several years believing that my own body was harboring a terrorist who could strike without warning. My lower back was always on orange alert.

Two things happened to change that. One, I found a book by Dr. John Sarno called *Healing Back Pain: The Mind Body Connection.* It could just as well have been called *Healing Back Pain: Does Tom Need to Be Hit Upside the Head with a Shovel?* I'd been having spasms the previous day, and I walked (carefully) into a bookstore at the local mall. For about twenty minutes, I sat on a hard wooden bench engrossed by Dr. Sarno's book. When I stood up, I swear to you, my back muscles had relaxed considerably. I was reading things I already knew. But only now was it really resonating.

It took the second thing to seal the deal. Before I share that story, I just want to take a moment to surrender any remaining dignity I may possess.

. . .

OK, I'm ready. (Who am I kidding? We're *way* past that point.)

It was just after Christmas in 2002. We were in New Hampshire, at McCree Manor. Earlier in the day, thinking an incline walk on a treadmill might ease some soreness in my back, I'd gone to the gym. The only thing that got a workout was my anxiety level. The frighteningly familiar prespasm tightness took hold within a few minutes of light exercise. That triggered the rapid-fire thought loop that only fueled the fire.

Oh no I'm going to have a spasm no I'm not don't think like that here it comes not yet oh shit breathe breathe breathe it's going to happen I just know it damn damn think about baseball . . .

Snow had fallen several days earlier, and area streets and sidewalks were an icy, slushy mess. After we returned from the health club, Lois suggested we go into town, where conditions were a bit better, and take a leisurely walk in the cold, fresh air. I agreed. Movement was better than sitting at home.

We parked on the main street. As I stepped up to the sidewalk just behind Lois, my right foot accidentally kicked the curb. That's all it took. My back seized.

Trying not to fall back into the slushy road, I grabbed on to her winter coat with both hands and held on tight. She couldn't move. I couldn't move. We looked like a statue of a mugging.

"Honey, try to stand up," she said. Her tone was amazingly calm given our ridiculous pose.

"Owww . . . can't . . . shit," I replied.

As best she could, given her constrained range of motion, Lois looked around for someone to help. "How can there be no one out here?" she said, sounding a little less calm.

Then she spotted two young women in a car next to ours watching us with open mouths. She waved them over. They turned and looked the other way.

When they glanced back she waved them over again. As they started to ignore her a second time she yelled, "Get out of the damn car and help!" (This is why you always want the redhead on *your* side.)

Within seconds, they were standing next to us making stupid apologies. "We thought he was attacking you," one said.

"Thanks so much," Lois said. "Good reason to hide in the car."

She pointed to a nearby restaurant. "Go in there and get a chair." They stared at her like she was speaking gibberish. *"Now!"*

They sprang into action as if they were veterans at taking restaurant chairs onto slushy sidewalks. Or maybe they were just afraid of Lois. In any case, I soon relaxed my winter-coat death grip, and, as the spasm passed, I sat on the borrowed seat.

As I did, still wincing through rapid, shallow breaths, one of the Dingbat Twins said to me, "Hey, you're that guy on television."

I didn't hear Lois say anything, but I can only imagine the look she gave them. Within seconds I heard their car engine start.

That night, after an uncomfortable but spasm-free few hours, I finally went to bed. At about one in the morning I woke up. Then I sneezed.

"FFFFUUUCCKKK!!!!!!"

It was even worse than that first spasm in the summer of 1998.

I grabbed the bedding like a life line and froze in place. For some reason, this spasm wasn't following the old pattern. Usually they'd hit and then, after a few long seconds, the muscles would relax. Not this time. This one just kept going.

By the time it *did* subside I was really rattled. After about fifteen minutes of watching me clutching the blankets, Lois said, "You should try to move."

"I can't," I whimpered. And for about an hour, I didn't.

But then I had to pee.

Ever so slowly, and with several stabs of pain, I made my way to the carpeted bedroom floor. With Lois at my side, I crawled on all fours toward the bathroom. The moment my hand moved from the warmth of the carpet to the cold tile of the bathroom floor, another massive spasm hit.

And then Lois spoke the words that completely changed my life.

"Honey, you can pee in the tub."

The moment she said that, I had an out-of-body experience. I imagined myself, a frightened forty-seven-year-old man, climbing into a bathtub to urinate. No way. That just wasn't going to happen. I refused to get pissed on. Finally, after being cowed by these spasms for over four years, I—was—pissed—off!

As Lois watched both in horror and amazement, I stood up.

I told a version of this story a few months later when I was a guest on *The View*. This next part I made PG for them. For you, here's the unedited version.

The short-fused, hot-tempered Tom whom I'd meditated into submission over the years suddenly came roaring back full-force like an avenging angel. *Enough with this bullshit! I'm . . . standing . . . up!*

As I did, another spasm attempted to buckle my knees. *Bring it on, you bastard! You damn . . . crap . . . fuck! Ow!! Shit!* I kept standing, moving through the pain for the first time. My back seized again. Then, dispensing with curse words, I simply began to roar.

Arrrrrrrrgh! I—am—standing—UP!!

Lois told me later it was like watching the Tourette's version of *Invasion of the Body Snatchers*.

As I reached my full, furious, five-foot nine-inch height, I was suffused with a sense of power I'd never felt before. I had made that back spasm my bitch.

I walked like Frankenstein's monster into the bathroom and peed. Standing up. Into the toilet (mostly). Accuracy wasn't the point.

Returning to the bedroom but not to the bed, I began to challenge the back spasms out loud.

"I'm bending over for my jeans, you sonuvabitch. Come on. Hit me."

Of course one did, but I roared through that one, too.

Then I moved to the center of the room, where there was nothing to grab on to. Lois was sitting on the bed by this point, wishing she had popcorn. "I'm going to touch my toes, you prick. Try to knock me over."

Another spasm. Another roar. I touched my toes and stood back up.

This went on for a while—me challenging the back spasms with another potentially painful maneuver, and the spasms, which had held me hostage for almost four years, trying to oblige. But even they couldn't compete with the sheer stubbornness of my rage. Eventually, they surrendered and I collapsed exhausted but victorious into bed.

"Well, that sure was something," Lois said dryly. And then we went to sleep.

I'd done it. I'd pushed through the pain. I had drawn a line in the carpet and refused to pee in the tub. I was immensely proud of myself. Of course, as Lois reminded me, this carnival side show of pain tolerance wasn't all *that* special. Women do it all the time. It's called "having a baby." And they tend to use more inventive curse words.

After that night in 2002, the frequency of the spasms diminished. When they came they still hurt like hell, but I wasn't afraid of them anymore. I knew I could handle them. My lack of fear made all the difference.

Here's what I finally realized (with help from Dr. Sarno and my wife). Absent any structural problem or physical injury (and the

MRI showed that my merry-go-round mishap hadn't left a scar), everything in my back was happening in my head.

Lois and I had made the decision *not* to relocate so as not to uproot the girls from their schools and their friends. But while *we* didn't relocate, *I* did. Initially, when I was only taping *Hollywood Squares,* it was for only a few days every other week. No biggie. But then, as I began adding things like *America's Funniest Home Videos*—and for another reason I'll get to in a few pages—the separations got longer. I kept telling myself that everything was fine, but my back kept reminding me that I missed my family. A lot. In hindsight, I realized how blatant the connection was. The spasms always hit within days of my boarding a plane. But since I wasn't dealing with the stress honestly, Newton's Third Law of Motion came into play.

For every action (*in this case, denying my feelings*) there is an equal and opposite reaction (*the back spasms*). Energy doesn't disappear. It just relocates.

As my occasional spasms and I flew to Los Angeles in the summer of 1998 to begin production of *Squares,* I began a new stage in my broadcasting career. I was literally "going Hollywood." And, to paraphrase the gang in Oz, my Walk of (moderate) Fame was about to be paved with fox-trots and crotch hits and games.

Oh my.

26

TIC-TAC-TOE-HOLD

MAY 19, 2000. NEW YORK CITY. DICK CLARK CALLED TO ME AS Lois and I were leaving the Daytime Emmy Awards preshow dinner. "Good luck tonight," he said.

I rolled my eyes. "Right. I don't have a chance in hell."

He laughed sympathetically. "OK, maybe next year."

As we got to our seats in Radio City Music Hall, one thing seemed certain. I wouldn't be getting up again during the show unless it was to go to the bathroom. Regis Philbin, whose *Who Wants to be a Millionaire* was providing a massive lifeline for the struggling ABC network, was a lock to win the Daytime Emmy as Outstanding Game Show Host. Because no category for game-show host existed in the Primetime Emmys, Regis was entered in the Daytime version. It was like inviting an eight-hundred-pound gorilla to your tea party.

Dick, who was producing the broadcast, had kindly acknowledged the fact that I was nominated for hosting *Hollywood Squares.* But even he, schooled as he is in the care and feeding of fragile show-business egos, couldn't keep up the pretense that I actually had a shot at winning.

Talking to my parents by phone that afternoon, I'd assured my dad that he could go to bed at his usual time. "Really, there's no point in staying up. Regis is going to win. Next time I visit I'll show you my 'I'm so happy for you' smile. I've been practicing."

As any awards-show devotee knows, watching the losing nominees' reactions is good, voyeuristic fun. Just the possibility of seeing
an impolitic *"This is bullshit!"* expression on national television makes
sitting through the windy acceptance speeches worth it. But I had
the advantage of a foregone conclusion. When Regis's name was announced, I'd be ready.

Except that it *wasn't* announced, at least not at first. When the
envelope was opened, soap star A Martinez paused dramatically and
said, "There's a tie."

Suddenly the Murmuring Crowd button was pressed. *A tie?*

"The first Emmy goes to Bob Barker for *The Price Is Right.*"

The audience applauded warmly. Bob, who was recovering from
knee surgery, wasn't able to be there. *How nice that he tied with Regis,*
everyone in Radio City Music Hall thought. I'm not psychic. But I
know that's what *I* was thinking, too. Then came the bombshell.

"The next Emmy goes to Tom Bergeron for *Hollywood Squares.*"

Now they hit the Excuse Me? button.

I, along with everyone in the place, was stunned. I stood with an
expression of absolute befuddlement and moved toward the stage on
autopilot. Somewhere in the distance, outside the hollow echo of my
own disbelief, I heard a mixture of gasps, applause, and a few outraged boos.

My performing instinct kicked in. *Acknowledge the moment. Get a
laugh. Then get your ass off the stage before they change their minds.*

I took the Emmy from A Martinez and turned to face the packed
house. I exhaled. "I thought I was just here for the dinner," I said.

The audience laughed. Next I turned my attention to only one of
its members.

I found the person I was looking for a few feet away from me, in
the front row. "Don't feel bad, Regis," I said, holding the Emmy that
was supposed to be his. "Eisner's buying you the Statue of Liberty."

Michael Eisner was then the head of ABC's parent company, Disney. *Millionaire* had given ABC higher ratings and more buzz than

anything since the heyday of the Fonz. Regis's appeal was a large part of the equation. Invoking Eisner's name might have been too much of an inside joke, but it also got a laugh. And when I did, Regis graciously gave me a thumbs-up.

After acknowledging my debt to Whoopi and the team, I had one last line. "I also want to thank Tom Hanks, Julia Roberts, and the pope." I paused a beat and looked at a sea of puzzled faces. "I don't know any of them, but I'd really like to book them on *Hollywood Squares.*"

Another solid laugh. I thanked the audience, and, to significantly more applause than greeted my arrival, I made a beeline departure for the wings. As I was being ushered toward the pressroom backstage, several hosts of *The View,* on deck to present an upcoming award, congratulated me on mine. Either Lisa Ling or Joy Behar (I always get those two confused) asked if I'd be going to the party. *The party? What party? I wasn't invited to any party.* "Yeah, maybe," I said, as if I knew exactly what we were all talking about.

I've appeared on *The View* probably a dozen times since that night, through all their hosting changes and soap operas, and it's pretty much a mutual admiration society. I love doing the show, and they keep inviting me back. But what made their enthusiastic party inquiry especially sweet in 2000 was something that had happened a year earlier at the 1999 Daytime Emmys.

One of *The View*'s producers, Sue Solomon, had approached Pat Lee, one of *Hollywood Squares* executive producers, and said she wanted to book me on the show. I'd been nominated that year, too (but lost), and had begun to get a little more notice in the business than from anything I'd done previously. When Pat relayed the request to me, I said I'd love to do it.

Weeks went by and I heard nothing more. Finally, I called Pat to ask what had happened.

"It's kind of funny, actually," Pat began. "When Sue pitched you as a guest they were all excited at first."

"What do you mean 'at first'?"

"They thought she was pitching Tom Berenger."

Trust me, it's hard to get a fat head with a malnourished ego. When they finally did book Tom *Bergeron* after his surprise Emmy win, he made sure to tell that story on their show.

The pressroom backstage at Radio City was a blast. I was peppered with a dozen variations on "Were you surprised?"

"Are you kidding?" I said. "I don't know who the judges were or what they were drinking, but I'll take this."

I mentioned that Regis had given me a thumbs-up. Someone said, "Are you sure it was a thumb?"

In the hotel room later, Lois asked me if I'd prepared the comments about the Statue of Liberty and the pope.

"I did," I admitted. "Everything except the 'I thought I was just here for the dinner' line. That was an ad-lib. I never expected to use any of it, but I wanted to have something ready just in case."

A couple of times that night I woke up and checked to see if the Emmy was really there. I was a little embarrassed by how lit up I was over it. It was an honor to be nominated and all that, but a whole lot sweeter to win.

Especially since during my first few *Hollywood Squares* tapings in 1998 I wasn't looking much like Outstanding Game Show Host material. Just ask those first contestants. While they were waiting for a chance to win some big money or exotic trips, I was having the time of my life still hosting a talk show.

Veteran game-show producer Steve Radosh, whom I referred to on the air as "Skippy Trebek, Alex's long-lost half-brother" (for no other reason than for my own amusement), offered some sage advice.

"I know it's tempting to engage all of the stars in conversation," he said, "but your main job is to take care of the contestants."

That was my game-show *aha!* moment. Once I shifted my focus and energy to them, I adapted much easier to my new job description. What's more, my comedic instincts became sharper as the pace of the show improved. I'd use Steve's advice later on *Dancing with the*

Stars as well, often becoming a sarcastic shield between our judges and the exhausted couples.

The contestants on *Hollywood Squares,* for the most part, had no problem keeping their priorities straight. They were in it to win it. There was no time to be starstruck. When Robin Williams taped several shows, I was surprised at how seldom the contestants called on him. Skippy, I mean *Steve,* pointed out that they knew Robin might go off on an improv riff that would take time away from the game. Less game equals less bounty. It was safer to go with someone like Gilbert Gottfried, my favorite "square" during our six-year run, who excelled at getting a quick laugh and giving a quick answer.

I specified "for the most part" because we did have our share of tic-tac-toe-impaired players. One of my favorites, who missed an easy win because he didn't go for his blatantly obvious third *X*, said by way of explanation, "I knew where I wanted to go. I just didn't know where I *was.*"

A prime candidate for a meditation class, I thought at the time.

Two players, described to me beforehand as teachers who would christen "Teacher Tuesday," made me wonder where the hell *I* was.

I was told that a number of markets were preempting *Hollywood Squares* for several Tuesdays in late March and early April because of the NCAA basketball coverage of the Sweet Sixteen through the Final Four. As a result, the producers wanted to have "stand-alone" shows where contestants appeared for only one day. Our usual format had the previous day's winner returning to face a new challenger. "Teacher Tuesday" was a way to explain the hiccup in our continuity and keep viewers in the NCAA markets from missing the ongoing competition. It sounded perfectly reasonable to me.

Except that it was all a lie.

The "teachers" were actors. "Teacher Tuesday" was a smoke screen to keep me from considering the airdate of the show. We taped shows several weeks in advance. This one would air on April 1. *April Fools' Day.*

The show started normally. I introduced the two contestants. In the *O* position was a sweet and slightly nervous young woman who told me she taught math at a junior high school. Her name was Carrie Armstrong. In the *X* position was an Oliver Hardy look-alike and self-proclaimed science teacher named Ed Bell.

After a few questions, both contestants began acting strange. Ed mumbled, "That's just dumb" after a Brad Garrett answer, and Carrie pleaded, "Don't yell at me" after some comic bullying by Penn Gillette of Penn and Teller. Ed, who seemed jacked up on triple espressos, began cheering at odd moments and sneering at Carrie. Carrie's eyes continued to widen, and she looked like she was starting to hyperventilate.

A little later, after I'd turned to the camera and said, "Some weeks they don't pay me enough," Carrie broke down crying and Ed taunted her for "folding like a cheap card table."

Lois, who was visiting the set that day with our daughters, told me that at the start of the show she was quickly ushered into the control room, where she couldn't catch my eye and tip me off to the joke. Not that she would have.

"He's not going to stop," Henry Winkler said to Lois as I continued to quip my way past the contestant minefield. Henry, along with Michael Levitt, had taken the reins of *Hollywood Squares* in season five. The Fonz had expected *me* to fold much sooner.

"You're right," Lois said. "He'll keep going." She knew me too well. I love it when all hell breaks loose. I was just trying to get enough of this bizarre show on tape so that we could air it.

Suddenly, with weeping and yelling going on all around me, a familiar voice boomed over the studio speakers. "Hey, Tom," Henry said, "April Fools."

For a moment, I was a deer in headlights. Then I looked offstage at producer Steve Radosh and asked, "Is the airdate for this April 1?" He nodded. At that I yelled "Brilliant!" and turned to congratulate the bogus contestants. Other cameras caught a number of the stars, who also had been fooled, applauding Carrie's and Ed's performances.

At lunch, Penn told me, "Teller and I have been fooling people for years. They even fooled *us.*"

You know what I learned from that? Never turn your back on Henry Winkler.

See if you don't agree with me. Some highlights of the show are at this link: http://www.youtube.com/watch?v=E0dkasKa7Yw.

Most of my fond memories of *Hollywood Squares* aren't from what happened on the air. Since we ended production in May of 2004, I find it's the off-camera moments I think of most often. Here are a few of them.

In January of 1999, a few months after the show's highly successful launch, Whoopi and I were in New Orleans to promote the show at the NATPE (National Association of Television Program Executives) convention. Our area, part of the larger King World exhibit, was a popular destination for convention goers. At one point, a "press availability" was scheduled, and dozens of photographers assembled. The explosion of flashbulbs as Whoopi and I stood before them was blinding and surreal. This was just another day at the office for my Oscar-winning friend, but for me it was startling. During a brief lull in the light show, actor-director Robert Townsend stopped by to say hi to Whoopi. The photographers yelled for a shot of the two of them together, and, as I began to step away, Whoopi shot me a look and said, "Get over here." She took my hand and pulled me back to her side.

One photographer, less than five feet away from me to my right, didn't share Whoopi's desire for my presence.

"Don't worry," he reassured the others loudly, "I can cut out the white guy."

During the show's first season Whoopi was dating actor Frank Langella, who played Perry White in *Superman Returns*, Richard Nixon in the Broadway and film versions of *Frost/Nixon*, and, years earlier, also onstage and on film, Count Dracula. He's an imposing guy, larger than life. And he hated my ties.

"Frank was acting all strange the other day," Whoopi told me at one of our tapings. "He said he had to go out, but he wouldn't tell me why."

"Really?" I said. I wasn't sure what this had to do with me.

"I finally got it out of him. He was going to buy you some ties."

Count Dracula was buying me neckwear? I was flattered but uneasy. Then I got a look at them and I was *really* uneasy. I think I may have worn one or two, but, to my great relief, he and Whoopi broke up not long after. I know that sounds callous of me, but you should've seen the ties.

There was the time I dragged my friend John Ritter backstage to see an old crate that had the logo from *The Jack Benny Show* on its side. We stood there gawking like we'd found the Holy Grail. John and I both loved Benny. He had taped his classic show on the same stage as *Squares.* This old box full of cables was the last remaining evidence.

Once, during our lunch break, I beat Venus and Serena Williams back-to-back in competition. Not on the courts; on a video game. Hydro-Thunder. "Care to try us at tennis?" Serena asked. I smiled politely and quit while I was ahead.

During another lunch, four of us sat talking while we balanced our lunch plates on our laps. There were Harvey Korman, Tim Conway, Carol Burnett, and *me.* I was in heaven. I peppered them with questions about their years together on *The Carol Burnett Show*, one of television's true gems. At one point I asked Carol about the odd half season after Harvey left the show and was replaced by, of all people, Dick Van Dyke. Even as a twenty-two-year-old DJ in Haverhill, Massachusetts, and a fan of them both, I thought it was an odd move.

"It didn't really work out," Carol said diplomatically.

Harvey was more direct. "You needed a Jew."

There were the many posttaping gatherings in the bar in the Century

City hotel where most of us East Coasters stayed. Usually it was me, Gilbert Gottfried, writer Dave Boone, and Jay Redack, a senior producer on our version of *Squares* who had written for Paul Lynde among others on the classic original incarnation. I often joked that Gilbert was the first to be cut off by the bartender—and he was only drinking water.

And speaking of the original show, known as *The Hollywood Squares,* there was the week of shows when our center square was none other than the original host, Peter Marshall. For one of those we swapped places and he once again became the host. He never missed a beat. As I watched him up there, I felt a mixture of admiration and job insecurity.

The other highlights of hosting a game show were exactly as Pat Sajak had described them to me years earlier in Boston on *People Are Talking.* You did a week's worth of work in a day. You helped total strangers fatten their wallets. You didn't even have to dress yourself; a new suit was hanging in your dressing-room closet after every show. Then, you got on a plane and headed home. Pat, like me, worked out west but lived back east.

After one such taping day I boarded United flight 16 at LAX at 6:50 p.m. on a Monday night for a planned 7:20 flight to New York's JFK airport. I was in first class, in seat 2C. I noticed Alan Cumming, who had won a Best Actor Tony Award in 1998 for his role as the Emcee in the revival of *Cabaret* (and who hadn't yet become Nightcrawler in an X-Men movie), sitting across the aisle in the first row. It was an uneventful flight, and I managed to sleep for part of it. Sometime after 3 a.m. Eastern Time, as we made our final descent to land, I looked out the window. There wasn't a cloud in the starry sky. The welcoming Manhattan skyline was visible through the windows to my right. It looked like the sun would rise to a beautiful late-summer morning. Not that I would see the sunrise. I wouldn't get home to Connecticut until close to 5 a.m. I planned on being sound asleep until at least 11.

But I wasn't. The phone rang and woke me a little after 10. My sister was on the line, in tears.

"I didn't know where you were. I didn't know if you were on one of the planes."

"I got in this morning," I said groggily. "What's wrong?"

"Turn on the TV. One of the towers already collapsed."

I reached for the remote and, minutes later, saw the north tower of the World Trade Center cave in on itself.

The beautiful late-summer morning was over.

27

GAME CHANGER

SEVERAL TIMES DURING THE SUMMER OF 2001, I'D LEFT OUR house in New Hampshire to drive to Boston's Logan Airport. From there I flew to L.A. for a weekend of taping *Hollywood Squares.* I always flew United Airlines. And from Boston, my flight of choice was United 175. It left around 8 a.m. and arrived in L.A. around 11 a.m. Pacific Time. But not on September 11, 2001. On that morning, terrorists plowed United 175 into the south tower of the World Trade Center.

In the months that followed, I'd occasionally look at pictures of the doomed flight crew and see if I could match them with my memories of warm hellos and friendly conversations by the cockpit door during my trips. I also wondered if one of those flights was among the scouting trips the hijackers took to determine how best to mount their attack.

By midday on September 11, Lois and I joined a long line of parents taking their kids out of school early. Then, with our next-door neighbors following us, we drove to our house in New Hampshire. Better to go there, far from Ground Zero, we reasoned, than stay in Connecticut, where we could see the billowing smoke of the attack site from the local beach on Long Island Sound. If that morning was to be only the first wave of a prolonged terrorist attack, New Hampshire seemed a much more unlikely next target.

The highway volume was eerily light, although we noticed a greatly heightened police presence along the way. Lois and I listened to news reports for some of the four-hour drive but then turned off the radio and continued in silence, communicating instead by occasionally squeezing each other's hand. In the backseat, the girls had their headphones on as their CD players offered a welcome distraction.

That night we all had dinner at a restaurant/pub in Portsmouth. The television over the bar provided the latest updates from CNN. A woman I didn't recognize approached our table. She seemed to be several drinks into the evening.

"I bet you don't remember me," she began. Her tone made it more of a challenge than a statement. I really wasn't in the mood for this.

"I'm sorry, I don't."

"I was your neighbor in Newburyport. You were upset at our dog barking."

While she still didn't look any more familiar, I did remember the dog. On the eve of my trip to Chicago to do clumsy magic tricks at a trade show (the gig booked by Tommy Tucker), the neighbor's dog was setting a *Guinness Book* record for nonstop barking. Unable to sleep (and in an anxiety-fueled temper tantrum), I stormed next door and, in no uncertain terms, offered to put their dog out of *my* misery.

I looked at her as she waited by our table for my reaction. "Oh, right," I said. Then I said nothing.

She stood there for a moment, clearly expecting more from me, then huffed, "Well, have a good night," and stormed away.

As we were leaving the restaurant we passed her table. I offered a flat "Good night" to her party and was met with glares. Lois, who was going to meet us on the sidewalk after a trip to the ladies' room, had a more animated interaction. She exited the restaurant looking furious.

"I don't believe those people," she said.

"The old neighbor?" I asked. "I didn't mean to be rude. I just couldn't do the whole 'You don't remember me' bullshit with her."

"As I was passing their table," Lois continued, "that woman said, 'What's *his* problem?' I said to her, 'Have you been watching the news? He's upset. *Everyone* is upset.'"

"She didn't get it?" I asked.

Lois shook her head in disbelief. "She said, 'Oh, please, that's all over with.'"

That's all over with? It had happened less than twelve hours earlier. I didn't know whether to be angry with her utter cluelessness or envious of it. I settled for mild disgust.

My next trip to Los Angeles to tape *Squares* was less than two weeks away. Though all flights were canceled for several days after 9/11, they were ready, albeit with major new security procedures, by the time I was scheduled to fly. But I, like a great many people, wasn't even remotely ready to fly. And, once I *did* get to L.A., however I got there, I wouldn't be ready to fly back.

Knowing that this new anxiety would require longer West Coast stays, I asked *Hollywood Squares'* business-affairs person about the possibility of getting a corporate apartment rather than a hotel room. She agreed that it was a good idea. She suggested I Web-surf for a few possibilities and we could look at them together after the next taping days. The taping days I didn't want to fly out for.

Lucky for me I had a friend with a decked-out bus whose fear of flying predated 9/11. Whoopi. And also lucky for me was that while Whoopi was at her new place in Malibu, her bus, having just brought several of her now also flight-leery relatives back home to New York, was available for me to use.

"It's got to come back here anyway," Whoopi told me. "Why don't you hop on?" She didn't have to ask twice.

I mentioned my impending bus trip to one of the producers at CBS's *The Early Show,* where I was occasionally filling in for Bryant Gumbel, and she had a suggestion. "During the trip," she said, "what if you do several stories on how Americans living far from the attack sites are dealing with 9/11?"

Almost all of the media focus, understandably, had been in New York, Pennsylvania, and Washington, D.C., where the hijacked jets had crashed. This was an opportunity to get a more personal reaction from the middle of the country. After mulling it over for a bit, and once Whoopi OK'd my adding some time and miles to the trip, I agreed to do it. I'm glad I did.

On Wednesday morning, September 19, a CBS News producer, John D'Amelio, met up with Whoopi's two drivers and me in a supermarket parking lot in Connecticut. I did my first *Early Show* report there, with the bus as my backdrop. I was completely honest about why I was taking the bus. I was too scared to fly. Back at the Manhattan studio, anchor Jane Clayson showed viewers a map of our planned route.

Over the next two days we talked with people at a truck stop in Des Moines, Iowa, and watched the president's address to a joint session of Congress alongside a cul-de-sac full of neighbors at a home in Englewood, Colorado. It was clear that for all of these people, unlike the woman at the restaurant in Portsmouth, New Hampshire, it would likely never be "all over with." It didn't matter whether they lived one mile or two thousand from where their fellow Americans died; the shock was evident, and the grief was shared.

By the time the bus dropped me off Friday afternoon at CBS Television City in Los Angeles, where *Hollywood Squares* was taped, I couldn't imagine how, the next morning, I'd go back to playing tic-tac-toe and cracking jokes with celebrities.

Before the first show taped on Saturday, Whoopi addressed the audience. She acknowledged how strange it felt to go back in the game-show bubble; to try to be funny so soon after the attacks had shaken our feelings of normalcy and security. Then she promised the audience, which had shown up in spite of all that, that we'd do our best to give them a "time-out" so they could, at least for a few hours, laugh again. She was wonderful. She put clearly into words what was a jumble in our gut.

The energy exchanged between all of us on the stage and the people in the audience that day was amazing. We wanted to entertain them, and they wanted us to know how much they appreciated it. We may not have been as funny as the laughs suggested or as deserving of the applause we received, but we all knew what we were really saying to each other. *We'll be all right. We'll get through this. And it's much better if we do it together.*

Togetherness, as far as Lois, the girls, and I were concerned, was about to be in shorter supply. With my anxiety about flying added to my increased workload—I started hosting *America's Funniest Home Videos* in early 2001—my time away from home was increasing. It still hadn't reached the critical mass where we'd reconsider the idea of moving everyone to California. It was just at the "more food for the back spasms" stage.

Which brings me to yet another rewrite of my favorite Zen fable:

There was once a family man who had a great job, which required traveling a great distance. One day he was offered another great job, also far from his home. Upon hearing the news, his neighbors came over to offer their congratulations. "Such good luck, except for the commute. That's got to be a bitch," they said. "You're right" was all the family man replied. A few months later, with both jobs going well, a terrible disaster struck not far from the man's home. "How awful," the neighbors exclaimed. "You're right," replied the man again. Soon after, the family man had a stabbing pain in his back that made him scream like a banshee. The neighbors offered their sympathy, saying again, "How awful." "You're right," whimpered the man. One night, the man, after declining a very tempting offer involving a bathtub, realized that his pain was connected to his love for his family. "How odd," his neighbors said. "You're right," the man replied again. His neighbors, observing that over these many months the family man had consistently agreed with everything they said, asked him, "Is that healthy? Always being agreeable?" The family man replied, "Maybe. But I'm certainly beginning to doubt it."

It took quite a while for me to realize that my "everything is fine" facade wasn't making everything fine. It was a lie. Not a big lie, but an important one. September 11 underscored for me, as it did for millions, how important it is to live your life *now*, because nothing else is guaranteed. That, I'm sure, played a part in enabling me to finally, and theatrically, push through the back spasms and understand their source. It was only when I owned the ache that it began to disappear.

Funny how that works, ain't it?

I eventually got over my flying anxiety. It just took time. Interestingly, not long after 9/11, I got a chance to boldly go on the most amazing flight I'd ever taken.

I flew into the twenty-second century. On board the starship *Enterprise*.

28

COFFEE WITH THE CAPTAIN

WHOOPI AND I WERE WALKING THROUGH ENGINEERING AS I gestured toward a large, cylindrical object.

"This is where the Suliban came back from the future and fucked with the warp coil."

"Oh," she said, nodding as if this was a normal conversation.

Our tour guide, Rick Berman, turned to me and smiled. "So you watch the show?"

"I do," I said. "I like the premise. Part prequel, part sequel. It's a good idea."

"The show" was *Star Trek: Enterprise,* known simply as *Enterprise* in its first two seasons on the now-defunct UPN Network. It featured the exploits of Captain Jonathan Archer and the crew of the first starship *Enterprise,* set about one hundred years before the arrival of Captain Kirk and Mr. Spock.

Rick had been head of the *Star Trek* franchise at Paramount Studios since the death of Gene Roddenberry, *Star Trek*'s creator, in 1991. Roddenberry died several years into the run of *Star Trek: The Next Generation,* which featured Patrick Stewart as *Enterprise* captain Jean-Luc Picard. Rick's tour of the new television show's sets was taking place during Whoopi's dinner break from shooting a cameo in the movie *Star Trek Nemesis,* the last of four films to feature the *Next Generation* cast. She was dressed as her character, a mysterious intergalactic bartender named Guinan.

After I'd praised the new show, Rick said, "Would you like to be on it?"

My brain raced. *Was I just offered a part on* Star Trek*? Could it be that easy?*

"Sure, I'd love to," I said casually.

He turned to Whoopi. "Can he act?"

Whoopi, who had seen me ad-lib like crazy on *Hollywood Squares* but never act, said, "Oh, yeah, he's very good."

Even *I* believed her.

Rick gave me his office number and told me to call. Then, after the tour, we hopped back onto his golf cart for the ride back to the *Star Trek Nemesis* set. I spent the rest of the evening watching a cold twenty-fourth-century Alaskan wedding reception being filmed on a hot twenty-first-century Californian soundstage. When I wasn't daydreaming about my own trip to the future, that is.

Several weeks went by before I got a call from the *Enterprise* production office to come by Paramount Studios for a costume fitting. I had no idea whether I'd be a Vulcan, a Klingon, or just some guy with antennae in the background of a crowd scene.

When I got there Robert Blackman, the show's costume designer, met me. "Pretty good," he said to me after we were introduced.

"What is?"

"Your part. Usually Rick has celebrities do little cameos. You're the whole opening scene."

Suddenly I was nervous. "I am?"

"I'm not supposed to do this," Robert said, "but I'll show you the script."

As he went off to grab his copy, I stood gaping at rows of futuristic clothing. *The whole opening scene?* Maybe Whoopi should have said, "Can Tom act? Oh, sure, about as well as Brando can fit into his old pants."

We looked at the script pages together when he returned. The episode was called "Oasis." My character, D'Marr, an alien trader of exotic goods, would be dining in the captain's mess along with Captain Archer (Scott Bakula), Chief Engineer Trip Tucker (Connor Trinneer), and Vulcan First Officer T'Pol (Jolene Blalock). Robert kept turning pages and D'Marr kept being on them. This was some meal they were going to have. It was already giving me indigestion.

For the first time since playing Johnny Casino in an outdoor summer production of *Grease* in New Hampshire in 1983 (a performance memorable only because I split my pants while singing "Hand Jive"), I had to learn lines!

After agreeing on what D'Marr would wear to dinner, I left Paramount with a copy of the script tucked under my arm. I vowed that by the day we shot the scene I'd be the best damn alien they'd ever seen. I'd be, if you'll pardon the pun, D'Marrvelous.

The morning of the shoot I arrived an hour ahead of my early-morning call time. I called Lois from my car, which had the Paramount parking lot pretty much to itself.

"You must be lit up like a Christmas tree," Lois said. She knew how much of a *Star Trek* fan I was, particularly of the movies featuring the original crew.

"I am," I admitted. "Hell, I'm claustrophobic, and I can't wait to sit still for hours while people glue latex appliances to my head."

And that's exactly what happened. It took four hours to glue on and spray-paint the turtle-head skullcap, neck gills, nose ridges, and other niceties that transformed me into D'Marr.

The shoot went smoothly. Scott Bakula set a calm, welcoming tone on the set. For me, this was a dream come true. For everybody else, it was just another day at the starship. That helped put me at ease, too. Plus, they all just assumed I could do this. Best not to let them down.

The four of us sat around the captain's dining-room table chatting about alien warlords, Triaxian silk, protein resequencers, and, as D'Marr had never tasted it before, coffee. The scene was shot a number of times. There was the master shot that included all of us, then our individual close-ups.

Once I knew I had my lines down cold, I set another goal for myself: break up the Vulcan. Jolene Blalock sat to my left fully in character, staring at me with the dispassionate expression of Mr. Spock's homeboys. From the moment she'd walked onto the set I hadn't seen her smile. I'd read that Leonard Nimoy was like that on the original *Trek*. It was pretty impressive. Finding the still point while meditating takes concentration. Finding it while wearing a wig and pointed ears takes real skill.

Not that I cared. I was on a mission.

When the camera was positioned for my close-up, I saw my chance. I thought it would be bad form to try to make her laugh during hers.

As the director called, "Action," Captain Archer, almost choking, asked D'Marr to name the fiery spice he'd brought for the meal.

"Haljaran," I said, turning to Jolene. "The warlords on Prios, or Preenos, or whatever the fuck planet they're from . . ."

She burst out laughing. Vulcans love it when you talk dirty.

When the scene was completed and the director announced I was released, Scott led the cast and crew in a round of applause for my performance. I was touched.

Then I came unglued. Actually, D'Marr did. What took four hours to create took only ninety minutes to disassemble. Then, alas, I was just me again, back in the Paramount parking lot, on planet Earth.

But while I had to leave the twenty-second century behind, I had plenty of space cadets in my future. And these life-forms, with their trampolines and piñata sticks and crotch hits, could make even a Vulcan laugh.

29

THE AGONY
AND THE ANNUITY

IF YOU EVER NEED A PARKING TICKET FIXED IN LATVIA, CALL ME. I'm very big in Latvia.

At least, that's what I was told by the winner of the Latvian edition of *Dancing with the Stars* when he visited our set in the spring of 2008. He wanted to interview me, but not because I was the celebrity ballroom host in the United States. He was a fan of *America's Funniest Home Videos.*

When Lois, the girls, and I were on a trip to England, a Danish family approached me for pictures and autographs as we sat on the top deck of a tour bus in Bath. Because of *America's Funniest Home Videos.*

But, lest you think the show's reach extends only to the European continent, think again. A friend recently told me that he was watching *America's Funniest Home Videos* on a small screen in the back of a taxicab. In Vietnam.

It could be that foreigners just love seeing Americans take one in the family jewels. But I think the show's appeal is much more basic and apolitical. *AFV*, as we hipsters call it, is usually silly, frequently stupid, and always funny. I think of it as a slapstick buffet.

We have another name for it at our house. The Annuity.

The nine years (and counting) I've spent as host of *AFV,* long enough to see my head of thick brown hair turn salt-and-pepper, is the longest I've spent at any job in my thirty-six years (ouch!) as a broadcaster. And, happily, it came about because I decided to go back home to Boston for one night.

The New England Emmy Awards, held in the capital of Red Sox Nation, is one of several regional versions of the Hollywood shindig. I've gone back to host the ceremony several times, most recently in 2006. But it was on May 7, 2000, one day after my forty-fifth birthday, that my pro bono hosting paid off big-time.

The New England Chapter of the Academy of Television Arts and Sciences—that's the fancy way to say "the Emmy people"—was honoring Vin Di Bona, the creator and executive producer of *America's Funniest Home Videos,* with a Lifetime Achievement Award.

Vin's television career also began at WBZ-TV (although he had left for California a few years before I arrived). One of his first jobs at WBZ was as a production assistant on the long-running weekend kids' show *Boomtown.* The live show, hosted by a genial singing cowboy named Rex Trailer, costarred Rex's palomino horse, Gold Rush.

"One of my responsibilities," Vin told me, "was to grab a shovel during the commercials and get rid of Gold Rush's shit."

What? And give up show business?

Vin and I knew each other casually. The last time I had seen him was in Los Angeles when I visited my friend Nancy Alspaugh, another WBZ-TV veteran, on the set of a show called *Richard Simmons' Dream Maker.* Nancy was the co–executive producer. Vin was executive producer. Richard Simmons, whom I had once sprayed with a water bottle labeled "Disco Sweat" when he got a little out of control on *Breakfast Time,* was the hyperactive host. The basic format involved a guest telling Richard what his or her dream was, Richard granting it, and then everybody crying. Richard cried at least five times an hour. His tear ducts deserved hazard pay. The show, despite its noble goals, lasted only one season.

While driving from Connecticut to Boston that day, I played with several ideas for opening lines. Beyond that, however, I was going to wing it. My approach to hosting the New England Emmys, or any other event, is no different than my approach to hosting *Dancing with the Stars*: be present, listen, and trust that opportunities are always in the air.

I work better in a reactive mode, playing off the unpredictability of the moment, which later created some challenges for me as I tried to adapt to *Videos'* largely scripted format. But on *that* night there was no script. I was making it up as I went along. And that's how I got the job.

The evening wasn't televised. It was essentially a formal dinner with prizes. From the moment the awards portion began I was, he says immodestly, in the zone. Every ad-lib hit the mark. Unbeknownst to me at the time, Vin's mother, Jean, who still claims I owe her 10 percent of my salary, turned to her son and said, "You should hire him." As I returned to our table after introducing another presenter, Vin, a dutiful son, leaned toward me.

"I want to ask you something," he said. "ABC is thinking of bringing *Funniest Videos* back to the schedule." It had spent two seasons as a series of specials hosted by various ABC sitcom stars. "Would you be interested in hosting it?"

"Sure," I said, "why not?"

Thus ended our brutal contract negotiation (except for some minor points my agent dealt with such as "How much you payin'?").

Actually, I had one more condition. All scripts would have to go through what I called a "de-Sagetization process." Bob Saget's style of hosting *America's Funniest Home Videos* was very different from how I'd be approaching the job. He came at it from the perspective of a stand-up comedian. I came at it from the perspective of a broadcaster. Bob and I talked about those differences not long ago when we both were guests on Penn Gillette's CBS radio show.

For example, when narrating the funny videos, Bob frequently used over-the-top cartoon voices. But when he was on camera he always kept a sardonic distance from the show. His expressions often conveyed a "What the hell am I doing here?" sensibility. *America's Funniest Home Videos,* like his sitcom *Full House,* contained all family-friendly G- or, at worst, PG-rated material. A Zen comedy coach (they're in the Yellow Pages) would say that those shows were very yin. They're like televised comfort food. Bob's actual sense of humor, despite the fact that he's a real mensch, is so yang, so out there, it could make Larry Flynt squirm. If you've seen his stand-up act, the film *The Aristocrats,* or his 2008 Comedy Central roast, you know what I mean.

Bob told me that that disconnect kept him from fully enjoying the incredible success of the show (which, by the way, my version has never matched, so he clearly was doing something right).

I, on the other hand, have always approached *AFV* from the standpoint of a host, not a performer. Well, not *always.* In at least a couple of my early shows, still haunting me in syndication, you can hear my pathetic attempts at Saget-like character voices. It didn't take long for us all to realize that funny voices weren't my strong suit. Even today, years later, if I stumble across one of those shows while channel surfing, I actually break into a sweat.

Bob, being a stand-up comic, wanted to score with a joke when he was on camera. In the show's early years they had elaborate sight gags and props to help accomplish that. As I saw it, my function was to get you to the clips. If I could get a laugh every so often, fine. But I was perfectly comfortable being the videos' straight man.

For me, there would be no sardonic distancing. I would embrace the deliberate cheesiness so tight I'd risk lactose intolerance.

Which didn't mean I hit the ground running. The de-Sagetization process took a while. If you were to ask head writer Todd Thicke (Alan's brother and Robin's uncle) about my early shows, he'd probably tell you I was swinging the pendulum too far in the other direc-

tion. I was so wary of sounding like Bob that I began jettisoning almost every joke. By the time I got through with a script, an Ingmar
Bergman film had more humor.

As Todd once put it to the writers as we sat down together for a
script meeting, "Here's where Tom kills your babies."

If you catch those early shows (look for a faux wooden floor on
the set and no gray hair on my head), you can watch me struggle
with finding the right tone. Some telltale signs include the rapid tossing of punch lines and excessive mugging to the camera.

Todd, along with a writing staff that included Mike Palleschi and
Trace Beaulieu (a veteran of *Mystery Science Theater 3000*), worked
along with me to find that tone. I didn't make it very easy on them.
For example, I had a few hard-and-fast rules. Among them:

I don't do wife jokes.

I don't do jokes at my kids' expense.

**I don't do jokes that require bogus recollections ("Just the other
day I was white-water rafting with a zebra when . . .")**

**I don't need a joke every time I'm on camera. A straight setup is
fine, too.**

My preference, as you've probably guessed by now, is to make
the joke at my own expense. But, when you host a show populated
by people throwing caution and their IQ to the wind, it's hard to
avoid spreading the wealth.

By this point, nine years in, the writers and I have grown so comfortable with each other that I hardly rewrite at all. And I'm much
more flexible on rule number three. After all, white-water rafting
with a zebra *is* a funny visual.

The one area of discomfort that still exists, for practically the entire staff, is the air temperature in the studio. It's cold. And it's *my* fault.

Nothing is worse for keeping an audience (or a host) alert than a warm studio. Plus, once I begin sweating, I turn into Albert Brooks's character from the film *Broadcast News*. My head is like an open faucet. Knowing this, I had a ready answer for Vin when he asked me, prior to my very first taping day in 2001, if there was anything I'd like to see in the studio to make my job easier.

"I'd like to see three things there," I told him. "My nipples and my breath."

One day that will go down in my sweat-stained history book is the day we shot the first two *AFV* shows of season sixteen, back in 2005. My call time at the studio wasn't until late afternoon, so that morning I met Carrie Ann Inaba, one of *Dancing with the Stars'* judges, at a Bikram yoga class. In case you're not familiar with this style of yoga, developed by Bikram Choudhury, it involves twenty-six postures and two breathing exercises spread over ninety minutes.

And, for your yogic pleasure, it all takes place in a humid room heated to 105 degrees.

The class was great except for the auctioneerlike chatter from the instructor. (Bikram likes the classrooms to be hot and, in my experience, the instructors to be annoying.) The heat and humidity, after the initial shock, provided a wonderful assist to my muscles as I attempted to twist into the various postures.

Unfortunately, the 105-degree heat is a gift that keeps on giving. Hours after the class, as I stood onstage preparing to kick off the new season, my internal organs were still trying, unsuccessfully, to cool down. The studio was cold, the staff offstage was bundled in sweaters and jackets, and I began to sweat. And then I began to *worry* about sweating. And then . . .

The faucet opened.

Every time I'd finish an intro and the videos began playing on the large screen in the studio, my makeup person ran to my side with tissues to blot my face, small sponges to reapply makeup, and repeated sighs to convey her displeasure.

"You probably shouldn't do any more hot-yoga classes on a show day," she advised.

Good call.

I noticed a number of people in the audience watching me with puzzled expressions during these perspiration pit stops. *What's he sweating about?* they were probably thinking. *This is a comedy show, not a tax audit.*

America's Funniest Home Videos, in its current incarnation, is a guilty pleasure. It's no longer the massive hit it was when it first appeared on the scene back in Bob's era. But it's remarkably durable, pulling in anywhere from eight to ten million people in its Sunday-night ABC network run, despite countless reruns on Superstation WGN and ABC Family. One would think that if you've seen one crotch hit or one hiccupping baby you've seen them all. As the show approaches its twentieth season, having already become ABC's longest-running prime-time entertainment program, one would be wrong.

In the spring of 2008, after one of *Dancing with the Stars'* results shows (the ones where we kick off a couple after making you wait an hour), I took a red-eye flight to Chicago to tape *The Oprah Winfrey Show.* Her topic? Unlocking the vault of *America's Funniest Home Videos.* In addition to myself, her guests were *30 Rock's* Tina Fey and *Saturday Night Live's* Amy Poehler, both such big fans of the show that they included a scene of their characters arguing over it in their film *Baby Mama.*

In the spring of 2009, as this book is appearing on store shelves, *AFV* is scheduled to be added to the Smithsonian Museum of American History alongside such iconic TV memorabilia as Fonzie's leather jacket and Archie Bunker's chair.

Stars such as Diane Lane and Kristen Bell have confessed in interviews to their addiction to *America's Funniest Home Videos.* At

Dancing with the Stars, Spice Girl Mel B, when she wasn't busy squeezing my butt (more about that later), begged me for DVDs of the show. *DWTS* season five champion Helio Castroneves told me he'd listed the show as a favorite on his bio, but his manager took it off.

"He said it wasn't cool enough." Helio shrugged. "He replaced it with *Friends.*"

One day, as I arrived at the studio for *Dancing with the Stars,* a staff member ran up to me as I was heading for my dressing room.

"Have you seen Dolly yet?" he asked. Dolly Parton was our musical guest that night.

"No, why?" I'd never met Dolly before and was looking forward to it.

"She's been asking for you."

I wasn't sure I'd heard him right. "She *has?*"

"Yeah, she wanted you to say hi when you got here."

Sweet. Dolly Parton wants to meet *me.* It felt a little backward, but what the hell. I immediately went into the ballroom where Dolly and her band were rehearsing. She saw me and yelled, in that adorable Dolly Parton twang, "Tom, I just love it when they put your head on other people's videos."

She was referring to a bit Todd and the writers had concocted a few seasons earlier called "Tom's Home Videos," or, as I often call it, "Bobblehead Tom." It was pretty simple to pull off. I sat on a stool for about fifteen minutes making faces while someone took pictures of me. Meanwhile, the writers and co-executive producer Michele Nasraway stood to the side yelling emotional cues. "You're angry." "You're giddy." "Something smells real bad." "You just saw Godzilla." They set up a database of all my expressions, digitally pasted any number of them on old videos, and, *voilà,* a recurring bit was born. Referring to the bit, *Entertainment Weekly* wrote, "We don't know what they were smoking when they came up with this but we want some."

When I'm out in public, the reactions I get from kids when they spot "the guy from *AFV*" are truly among my most enjoyable career bonuses. Perhaps that's how *you* know me. And I don't mind being *that guy. Dancing with the Stars* may be the bigger ratings success, the current pop-culture darling (after *American Idol*), but the silly pleasures of *America's Funniest Home Videos* have become a comfortable, dependable escape for millions. *AFV* is like macaroni and cheese. It isn't, as Helio Castroneves's manager said, trendy or cool. But every so often it's just what you need.

Back in 1981, when I got the job hosting *Super Kids* in Boston, WBZ-TV sports anchor Bob Lobel had told me, "You've got your foot in the door. Make yourself invaluable. Whatever they offer you, take it." With *America's Funniest Home Videos*, I had my foot in the door at ABC. So when Andrea Wong, then executive vice president of Alternative Programming at the network, came to me in 2003 with an offer to host a classic slice of Americana, I said yes.

However, I was about to move my foot from the doorway to my mouth. And, in the process, I'd piss off the entire Miss America Organization, too.

So before we get to the ballroom and *Dancing with the Stars,* let's take a detour to Atlantic City.

30

SOMETHING'S AMISS AMERICA

WHAT THE HELL DID YOU SAY THIS MORNING?" MY AGENT, Babette Perry, asked me. "I just got off the phone with the Miss America people. They were furious."

I had to admit I saw this coming. "I was on *Ali & Jack* [*Living It Up! With Ali & Jack,* a short-lived live talk show hosted by Ali Wentworth and Jack Ford], and I told that story about the dress rehearsal."

"Not the one with the neck massage?" she said nervously.

"That's the one."

There was a pause on the line. Then she said, "Oh, shit."

Saying yes to hosting the Miss America Pageant wasn't my easiest decision. As a father of two daughters, I wasn't sure that presiding over a swimsuit contest, whether they called it a "scholarship competition" or not, would be sending them the right message. But they were the ones who talked me into it.

Jessica, then almost fifteen, put it this way: "Dad, we get it. We're not going to suddenly try to become Miss Connecticut. It's just a show. And it's live. You love that. That's why they asked you."

Samantha, almost thirteen, agreed: "You should do it. Mom can go to Atlantic City with you. You'll have fun."

Once that was settled, all that was left was negotiating the deal and announcing Miss America's new host to the press. As part of the announcement, I was asked to do several interviews. One was with

Associated Press reporter John Curran. As you'll see, despite my daughters' OK, it's clear that their dad was still wrestling with his decision. Or at the very least that I should have meditated that morning and focused my attention.

Here's an excerpt from the interview.

Tom Bergeron, host of "Hollywood Squares" and "America's Funniest Home Videos," will be master of ceremonies at this year's Miss America pageant telecast.

Bergeron said he's happy to sign on with the world's most famous beauty pageant, even if it isn't the freshest thing on network TV.

"I referee a tic-tac-toe game, and I introduce clips of people hitting themselves in the (groin). This will help my career, if anything," he said.

The pageant airs live Sept. 20 on ABC.

"Even if it isn't the freshest thing on TV?"

Jesus, Tom, it's OK to THINK that, but did you actually have to SAY it out loud? TO A REPORTER??

"This will help my career, if anything?"

Oh, real smooth. And, also worth noting, the reporter did you a favor and scrubbed up another one of your quotes. You didn't say, "Groin." What you really said was, "I introduce clips of people hitting themselves in the NUTS!"

Poetry, Tom, pure poetry.

The full interview, which prompted the *first* outraged call to my agent from the Miss America Organization, included other gems along the lines of (and I'm paraphrasing), "In a way it's a reality show like *Survivor*, with Atlantic City as the remote island. I get to watch a bunch of beauty queens all get voted off until we crown the winner. It should be fun." And then I added, "But I'm not singing that song."

I was referring to the signature tune, "There She Is, Miss America," that always accompanied the newly crowned winner's victory walk. They had a professional singer record it the year I hosted, freeing me to just smile and clap.

Let's examine a few of the ways my comments could have been interpreted.

You've compared the longtime home of the event to a deserted location where you're lucky if you can find firewood.

You've gleefully anticipated the emotional devastation that will befall at least forty-nine young women.

You sound like the tone-deaf demon spawn of Bert Parks.

Now, at the time, I just thought I was being funny. I couldn't understand why anyone would be upset with me.

Hello there, is that your baby in the stroller? It is? I'm sorry, SHE is. That's really a girl? Really? She's a little weird looking, don't you think? Seriously, have you ever taken a good look at her? Yowzhah! Hey, no need to take offense. I'm just kidding.

That's kind of the same thing.

At Babette's urging and because, once I saw my comments in print, I could understand why they were upset, I called the Miss America organizers and apologized. I assured them (with crossed fingers) that I had been misquoted.

Everything went fine from there. The pageant even dodged a natural disaster when Hurricane Isabel decided at the eleventh hour to veer off course from Atlantic City. The early forecasts had been scary enough that, during my opening monologue, I mentioned we had "encased the tiara in plywood."

There were several times during the live broadcast, which originated from the cavernous Boardwalk Hall, that I had to bite my tongue and smile politely. "The Miss America Quiz," where I posed questions to the contestants about current events, U.S. history, and U.S. government, was one of those times. I kept hearing David Letterman's voice in my head tempting me like a gap-toothed devil to unleash my inner snark. I behaved myself.

I did find a few milder, albeit punny, outlets for humor. When Miss Wisconsin, Tina Marie Sauerhammer, took the stage with her cello to perform a classical piece, I offered her as proof that "there's always room for cello."

But, as with most of the shows I've hosted, it was what happened off camera that provided my favorite memory. During our dress rehearsal on the afternoon of the broadcast I sat backstage making notes on the script. Suddenly I felt two soft, strong hands massaging my shoulders and neck. I turned to find a contestant from one of the southern states smiling at me mischievously.

I smiled back, although it may have looked more like a goofy grin. "That's a real nice neck massage," I said.

She squeezed a little tighter, pressing her palms into my shoulders. "And if I win," she said, her southern accent stretching out the last word, "I'll give you a full body massage."

Absolutely true story (no crossed fingers). And that's exactly how I told it weeks later on live, coast-to-coast morning television.

Babette laughed in spite of herself when I told her what I'd done. Still, she had some scolding to do. "I hope you didn't plan on hosting Miss America again."

No, actually, I didn't. I couldn't see myself *ever* hosting another competition involving gorgeous, scantily clad women.

Boy, was I wrong.

31

"MARCO," "POLO," AND WATTS

I WAS SECONDS AWAY FROM WALKING ONTO THE STAGE OF ATLAN-
tic City's Boardwalk Hall to host the live broadcast. There were thou-
sands of people in the hall and millions more watching at home.

My mind went blank.

I turned to my friend Dave Boone, the head writer on *Hollywood
Squares,* who'd worked with me on this show, too. We'd crafted much
of the opening monologue with jokes about the gathering storm that
had been threatening the pageant all week.

"What's the name of the hurricane?" I said in a panic.

"Isabel," he said. "Are you all right?"

I took a deep breath, trying to center myself. "I couldn't remember it. And we've been talking about it for days. That's not a good
sign."

"It's been a tough week," Dave said. And he wasn't talking about
the hurricane.

I had a comforting thought. "I'm going to imagine that John's
watching," I said. "This one's for him."

The 2003 Miss America Pageant took place in Atlantic City on
September 20, 2003. Nine days earlier, on September 11, our friend
John Ritter had died suddenly in Burbank, California, of an aortic
dissection. He had been rushed to a nearby hospital from the set of his
ABC hit, *8 Simple Rules.* It was his daughter Stella's fifth birthday.

Five days earlier, on September 15, Dave and I had been standing with a small group of family and friends at John's gravesite in Forest Lawn.

It had been a tough week indeed.

The morning of September 12, a Friday, I was at home in Connecticut getting ready to leave for a weekend of taping *Hollywood Squares.* A car was due to arrive within the hour to take me to JFK. I was in my office going over some bills when Lois, who had just logged on to her computer, cried out from the other room.

"Oh my god, Tom, John is dead."

I remember exactly how the impact of those words felt. My body absorbed them on dual tracks. My chest reacted like a weight had been dropped on it. My mind immediately tried to rewrite Lois's message. I was accepting and rejecting the news at the same time.

We sat together by her computer reading the news reports. One of John's best friends, Henry Winkler, whom I would see at *Squares* the next morning, had been rehearsing an episode of *8 Simple Rules* in which he was to play John's new boss. John had complained that he was tired and had left the set early. Henry thought he was really sneaking off to celebrate Stella's birthday. That's the last time they saw each other.

I flew to Los Angeles and drove to my Santa Monica apartment in a daze. Once there I decided to call and leave a message for Amy Yasbeck, John's wife, offering to do whatever I could to help. I expected to get their machine. Amy answered.

"I'm so sorry," I said. The words seemed weightless, but they were all I had.

She told me about the previous night, about learning that John had an aortic tear. "They did everything wrong," she said in describing his treatment. "They thought it was a heart attack. Everything they did just made it worse."

In March of 2008 a jury would clear John's attending physicians of wrongdoing by a nine-to-three vote. (Civil cases don't require a unanimous verdict.) Should other tests have been run to determine John's condition? Was there time? I don't know. I do know that however you answer those questions, it doesn't bring Stella's dad, Amy's husband, and my friend back.

A few months before John got *8 Simple Rules,* we were standing backstage at *Hollywood Squares* waiting to be introduced to the audience. He'd just finished reading an unpublished novel I'd written. I warned him, when he insisted I give him a copy, that there was a reason it had gone on what I called "the rejection-letter circuit." I was extremely flattered that he'd not only read it, but quoted dialogue from it verbatim. What's more, he wanted to work together to adapt it into a TV movie.

It was a comic novel about an alcoholic actor haunted by the ghost of his psychiatrist. It had a solid premise and a lousy third act. But it also had, as expressed by the ghostly shrink at one point, my actual feelings about an afterlife. The actor, resigned to being "accompanied" by the apparition, asks him to define heaven.

"Imagine you throw a rock into a pool," he answers, "and water explodes into the air from the force of the impact before falling back in. We are the water exploding into the air. We think we're unique. We think we're individuals. We're not. We're always just part of the pool. We fly up but never away. We're all linked."

"We go back to the pool. I really like that idea," John said.

I do too. But for me it's more than just an idea. When I meditate regularly, I *feel* it. The sensation of being pure energy, of being connected to a greater whole, is palpable.

Once, years ago, I was performing in Newburyport, Massachusetts, and taking improvisation cues from the audience. I'd ask one person to suggest a character ("You're a panhandler," "You're a circus clown") and another, from a different table, to suggest a situation for that character ("You're on a space ship," "You're trapped in a freezer"). From that I'd improvise a bit.

One night, after taking the two suggestions, I began to improvise.

It was electric. I felt like the jokes were being downloaded from some celestial database, like I had tapped into a comedic power grid. As I was performing, I glanced over to where my agent at the time was sitting. She was wide-eyed. When I finished, the audience applauded and whistled their approval. And then I made a fateful error. I took my ego out for a polishing.

I thought, *Wow! I'm really good. I killed!*

At which point I disconnected from the grid. My very next improvisation, performed only minutes after my crowd-pleaser, stunk up the room like a flatulent sumo wrestler.

The only difference between those two improvisations was my mind-set. In the first, I was open to the possibilities of the moment. I was listening. It wasn't about me. In the second, once my ego engaged, I was patting myself on the back so hard the noise drowned out everything else. The celestial download crashed.

I was brought up to believe that what we did in this brief hiccup of existence bought us an eternity of salvation or damnation. I could never wrap my head around that. Some people I know will be lucky if they learn how to text-message before they die, let alone figure out how to really communicate. Life goes fast. Eternity goes forever. The math seemed wrong. But the sensation of connection, of being all part of the same pool, always felt right.

Eastern philosopher and author Alan Watts, whose quote "If you hold your breath, you lose it" I shared with you earlier, has another saying I really like. It's drawn from Hindu myth, from the belief that all reality is a matter of coming and going. He said that we are all God, playing hide and seek with Himself.

That's not to say we should all develop a God complex. That's just for doctors and politicians. What he's saying, as I read it, is that we're all part of a greater whole, that we're not just an "ego inside a bag of skin."

When I think of John, of my teacher Tony Montanaro, or of any of the people close to me who've died over the years, I don't think of

them as having really gone. And I don't think of them eternally praying on a cloud or burning in a fire. They've just gone back to the pool.
They're just having a swim.

Every time I lose sight of that pool, every time my ego grabs the
controls (like onstage in Newburyport), I feel unplugged from the
grid. It's not always due to arrogance. My ego, like the rest of me,
sometimes grabs the controls out of confusion. And, also like the rest
of me, it stubbornly refuses to stop and ask for directions.

That's how I felt for the first season and a half of *Dancing with the
Stars.* As Tony would have described it, I was "off the deck," not quite
connecting to the experience.

Getting there would literally require some fancy footwork.

32

SIX WEEKS OF SEQUINS

BABETTE WAS ON THE PHONE WITH THAT "DON'T MESS WITH ME" tone to her voice. "ABC wants you to do a summer show," she said, "and you're going to do it."

I've heard that tone from her only three times over our more than twenty years together. That was one occasion; insisting I take the *Good Morning America* job was another. Writing this book was the third. Send any refund requests to her.

"What's the show?" I asked.

"It's live," she said, dodging the question. "You love live television."

I persisted. "But what's the show?"

"It's a big hit in England," she said.

"Right. What aren't you telling me?"

She paused. "Before you say no you have to promise to watch the British show. They're sending you a DVD."

I was curious enough by this point to agree to almost anything. "Fine, fine, I'll look at the British show. Just tell me, what kind of show is it?"

"A celebrity ballroom competition."

I'd said *almost* anything. "You're kidding."

"You promised," she said.

"Yes, I did. I will look at it before I say no. And *then* I'll say no."

The next day, the DVD arrived. In the interim, I told Lois about the crazy conversation I'd had with Babette.

"Can you get over that?" I said. "A celebrity ballroom show."

"You should do it," she said without hesitation.

I suspected collusion. "Have you been talking to her?"

"No, but she's right. Ballroom dancing is catching on. Several of my friends are taking classes, and that Richard Gere movie was wonderful."

The movie, *Shall We Dance,* was a romantic comedy starring Gere as a bored estate lawyer who gets one look at Jennifer Lopez and signs up for her ballroom-dance class. I had to admit I enjoyed it as well. Given that, along with Lois's and Babette's ringing endorsements for the idea, I was willing to watch the DVD with a (somewhat) open mind.

The BBC show, the mother ship for the numerous international versions of *Dancing with the Stars,* is titled *Strictly Come Dancing,* a clumsy grammatical marriage of *Come Dancing,* a ballroom-competition show that dates back to 1949, and *Strictly Ballroom,* a 1992 Australian film cowritten and directed by Baz Luhrmann. On the original, long-running, and, by the end, low-rated *Come Dancing* the competitors were, imagine this, actual ballroom dancers. In 2004, when the show was retitled and reformatted, it became a sequined celebrity reality show. *And* a massive hit for the BBC.

I put in the DVD and sat down to watch. Within ten minutes my resistance was wavering. Twenty minutes in I was hooked. And it wasn't just because of the dancing (or the almost nonexistent costumes on the women). What appealed to me, in addition to the fact that it was "LIIIIVE," was its whimsical split personality: part variety show, part reality show. The host, Bruce Forsyth, a British institution, brought a charming vaudevillian energy to the glitter-ball showdown. The celebrities, waltzing and fox-trotting for the first time in their lives (and on live television, no less), provided a compelling fish-out-of-water element. And, unlike a number of reality shows popular at the time, it didn't require any backbiting or bug eating by the contestants. Maybe Lois and Babette were right. This could be fun.

And, what the hell, it was only going to run for six weeks.

I called Babette. "OK," I said, "I'm in."

"Good," she said. "Now I don't have to kill you."

With my homicidal agent mollified and happily on her way to negotiate my contract, I had some delicate negotiations of my own to attend to. The first broadcast of *Dancing with the Stars* would be on June 1, 2005. I had a prior commitment on that date. I was scheduled to be back at my alma mater, Haverhill High School, to be the keynote speaker at my niece Allyson's senior chapel, the last assembly and award ceremony prior to graduation. I had been keynote speaker at her sister Katie's senior chapel several years earlier and had promised her I'd be there for hers, too. Some promises you really hate to break. This was one.

Not that I didn't have a novel excuse. *Hi, Ally. This is your uncle. I hate to pull a no-show, but I have to be in Los Angeles to introduce Evander Holyfield's cha-cha.*

She'd understand, of course. She'd seen how often work had pulled me away from other family gatherings over the years. Still, I wanted to make *some* kind of appearance, maybe break only half of a promise. So, a week before *Dancing's* debut, I drove to my hometown from Connecticut and taped an apology on the high school stage from which I'd been scheduled to deliver the keynote address. I explained that although I really wanted to be there, I was going to be hosting a live, network ballroom-dancing show. On cue several irate Haverhill High seniors, my niece included, appeared on either side of me.

Huffing that my apology was not only preposterous but also unacceptable, they picked up the podium and microphone and stalked offstage, leaving me standing there with nothing but a sheepish grin. I mimed a rope pull and made my exit.

Allyson told me that when the tape was played at senior chapel it got a great reception. And my guilty conscience got a reprieve.

The idea for the taped bit, for finding a way to make lemonade out of lemons, sprang from the same instinct that kept me quipping through the bizarre *Hollywood Squares* taping that turned out to be an April Fools joke.

What possibilities exist here? What is presenting itself to me IN THIS MOMENT that I can use? In a very real sense, it's meditation in motion, the practical application of an esoteric practice. And it relies on the acceptance of serendipity.

Serendipity, the effect of accidentally discovering something fortunate, is one of the key reasons I was offered the job hosting *Dancing with the Stars.* Although I had a good relationship with executives at ABC, the Brits from the BBC who would be producing *Dancing* didn't know Tom Bergeron from Tom Berenger. But one of their American executives, Linda Giambrone, did. We'd worked together on *Hollywood Squares.* As the British producers described what they were looking for in a host, Linda sat them down to watch the April Fools show from 2003. By the time they got up again, they thought they'd found their guy.

How many different puzzle pieces had to align to get me to the ballroom? If I hadn't decided to toss out the show outline when Whoopi visited *Fox After Breakfast* in 1996, we wouldn't have established the rapport that made my *Hollywood Squares* audition a slam-dunk in 1998. If I hadn't hosted the New England Emmy Awards in 2000 when Vin Di Bona was being honored, I wouldn't have been offered *America's Funniest Home Videos.* If I hadn't hosted *AFV* I wouldn't have established a relationship with the network. If, on *Hollywood Squares* in 2003, I'd asked to stop tape because the contestants were clearly whack jobs, there'd have been nothing for Linda to show the BBC producers in 2005.

I could easily weave a few more threads into this almost decade-long tapestry, but you get the idea. Everything is connected. That's the pure Zen of it.

With *America's Funniest Home Videos* wrapped for the season and not shooting again until August, *Dancing with the Stars* seemed like a fun way to spend part of my summer vacation. The possibility that it would be anything more never crossed my mind. Maybe, if it did well enough, it'd come back again for six weeks the following summer. That's about how lofty my expectations were. By July 7, however, once the ratings for the finale came in, it was clear I had to do some serious expectation reevaluation. As Steve Rogers wrote for the online Reality TV World,

> *ABC's* Dancing With The Stars *series ended its season with a bang on Wednesday night, drawing the most viewers and highest Adults 18–49 demographic numbers of any summer television series since Fox's September 2002 finale of* American Idol's *first season.*

Over twenty-two million people watched the controversial finale that saw our first mirror-ball trophy awarded to *General Hospital* star Kelly Monaco and her professional partner, Alec Mazo.

I'm not kidding about Kelly's win being controversial. Blame it on a slow news cycle or overactive conspiracy theorists, but when John O'Hurley (*Seinfeld*'s J. Peterman) and his elegant partner, Charlotte Jorgensen, came in second, it unleashed a spandex shit storm. Here's how the Associated Press reported the fallout.

BEVERLY HILLS, Calif.—Kelly Monaco knows there are television viewers who aren't happy she won ABC's "Dancing With the Stars" competition, but she isn't going to let it bother her.

"I do not hold anything personally. I'm not going to go home and cry because someone did not like my dancing," the actress from ABC's "General Hospital" said Tuesday of a viewer backlash.

"I felt from the beginning this is fun for me. . . . If you don't like it, you don't like it. I wouldn't be sitting here if the whole world hated what I did," she told the Television Critics Association.

Monaco and the producers of the ABC series were peppered with questions, with some reporters saying they received complaints from viewers who were confused by the voting process that relied on both the audience and judges.

Questions also were raised about possible network favoritism for Monaco. The runner-up was John O'Hurley, who played catalog king J. Peterman on NBC's "Seinfeld."

Judge Len Goodman said the results weren't influenced by the network.

"I never knew she was on ABC," he said of Monaco.

I love Len Goodman. We've done seven seasons now, and sometimes I'm not sure he knows *he's* on ABC. Just kidding. He must.

I found the whole brouhaha over Kelly's deserved win pretty silly. Yes, John and Charlotte were wonderful together, the picture of refined elegance. But Kelly and Alec, who endured some withering criticism from the judges in the first few weeks (Bruno Tonioli's "Is there a death in the family?" comes to mind), had remarkable tenacity, a sharp learning curve, and, in the end, more votes.

Serendipity was their friend, too. During their samba in week four, Kelly's wardrobe malfunctioned when the straps on her top popped. Instead of freaking out, she grasped, laughed, shrugged, and danced. For the first time all season, she had more "pressing" priorities than nailing the right steps. Paradoxically, it was her most relaxed performance and marked a major turnaround for her and Alec. Two weeks later their freestyle routine earned the season's only perfect score (three tens) from the judges.

"The moment I couldn't think about the steps anymore," Kelly told me, "my body took over and danced."

If you hold your breath, you lose it. But if you hold your top, you win it.

Until the rematch, anyway.

In September of 2005, both to address the controversy and to keep the show on people's radar, ABC aired *Dancing with the Stars: The Dance-off.* I had mixed feelings about it (although I happily cashed the check). To me, Kelly won fair and square. If you didn't like it, tough. Hey, I voted for Gore back in 2000. I'd learned how to swallow hard and move on.

John and Charlotte won the *Dance-off,* decided by viewer votes alone, by only one percentage point. As the phone votes were tallied, the producers told me Kelly and Alec were ahead in three out of four time zones, falling behind only at the end.

The show didn't come close to duplicating the ratings success of the first season finale. Using my twenty-twenty hindsight, here are my thoughts as to why:

By the time the *Dance-off* aired, most people in the viewing audience had moved on with their lives. What makes you crazy in July you often can't remember in September. Especially if it was only a TV show.

By its very nature, a rematch would be playing to only a portion of the original audience. Assuming half of that audience thought John and Charlotte won, not even all of *them* would show up for a ballroom mulligan.

Still, when the *Dance-off* Nielsen numbers came in, I began to wonder if the bloom was already off the *Dancing with the Stars* rose. Maybe this was only a summer show after all.

We wouldn't know for sure until January of 2006, when season two hit the airwaves. Everything was bigger: there were now ten couples competing over eight weeks, with an hourlong results show added to the mix. We kept our fingers crossed that the audience would be bigger, too.

And there was another change. My cohost, Lisa Canning, a former reporter for *Entertainment Tonight,* was replaced by Samantha Harris, a staple of the E! Entertainment Television channel.

While Lisa was undoubtedly personable and gorgeous, she appeared to find live television daunting. She's not alone. Most people in the business do. When I tell people, even longtime veterans in the business, that I *prefer* it, they often look at me like I'm nuts. And, in fairness to them, the jury is still out on that point.

Samantha's experience as a red-carpet reporter for *E!,* which involved conducting off-the-cuff live interviews with distracted celebrities, made her a logical choice for the job. It also didn't hurt that she, like Lisa, is a stunner.

In the same way the *Dance-off* gave John O'Hurley a second chance, *Dancing with the Stars* got one, too. The second-season premiere was a ratings smash. Utilizing my *Star Trek* reference guide, I told interviewers that the rematch occurred in "an alternate timeline" and the viewers clearly knew the difference. With a new batch of solid numbers, we were back to thinking we just might have a franchise here.

I often get asked, "Did you have any idea that *Dancing with the Stars* would be such a hit?"

Originally I always answered honestly. "Of course I didn't have any idea." But now, more often than not, I lie through my teeth.

"Yes, I definitely knew a celebrity ballroom competition would be massive. Just like I knew a show featuring groin hits and piñata injuries would pay for my kids' college education."

Screenwriter William Goldman famously said about Hollywood, "Nobody knows anything." That may be true about the people *making* the movies and television shows, but it's not true about the public. They know a lot about what they like and what they don't. And, in the age of the blogosphere, they're not bashful about telling you.

As season two began, I still wasn't comfortable with how I was hosting the show. That's a sentiment that was shared by quite a few viewers posting their critiques on message boards. "Send him back to *America's Funniest Home Videos*" was a common refrain.

When I mentioned the criticisms to co-executive producer Izzie Pick, she told me to ignore them. "Why are you reading those things anyway?" she asked.

"Maybe I'm a glutton for punishment," I told her. But it was more than that. I kept reading the scathing reviews because on some level I knew they were right. And until I could put my finger on how to fix it, I was drawn to the message boards like a moth to a flame.

And then I realized that Kelly Monaco, when talking about her own epiphany, had given me my answer, too. I should just stop thinking about it.

And dance.

33

A STEP IN TIME SAVES MINE

LOIS WAS SURE I WAS HAVING A HEART ATTACK.

She and the girls were spending a few days with me at our California home. Although I'd been feeling anxious about a situation at work, I was thrilled to be with my family. Everything about the night before had been perfectly normal. Then, at around 2 a.m., it happened.

I began thrashing about under the covers and, as Lois described it, hyperventilating, too. Memories of my food-poisoning scare from a decade earlier came rushing back to her. The paramedics. The ambulance ride. The frightening misdiagnosis: "He's going into cardiac arrest." The shot of adrenaline she'd stopped them from administering just in time. *Not again,* she thought.

She shook me. "Tom, wake up! Tom!"

My eyes blinked open. I was ecstatic. "I did it," I said. "I just danced all the steps!"

I wasn't having a heart attack. I was having a quickstep.

For the first time, after two weeks and countless hours of frustrating rehearsals, I'd managed, in a dream, to figure out all of the transitions, dance all the steps. I wasn't thrashing under the covers. I was dancing.

A few weeks into season two of *Dancing with the Stars* I decided to pitch an idea to one of our professional dancers, Ashly DelGrosso.

Ashly and her partner, Joey McIntyre (of New Kids on the Block), had been the first dancers on our first show of season one. She had become not only an audience favorite but one of mine as well. Her season-two partner, rapper Master P, was proving a bit of a challenge. He had joined the cast as a last-minute replacement for his son, Lil' Romeo, who, we were told, had injured himself playing basketball.

Stepping in for his son was the last discernible step Master P made. Watching poor Ashly try to maneuver the lumbering hip-hopper across the dance floor was like watching someone try to move furniture to music. She was a great sport and a total pro, never complaining once that her partner was woefully unsuited for ballroom dancing.

Which were just the qualities I'd be counting on.

"When you two are voted off," I asked her, which for her sake I hoped would happen sooner rather than later, "would you be willing to dance with me?"

Talk about a frying-pan-to-fire scenario. But she said yes. In fact, she said, "I'd love to."

Now that I had a partner, I just needed permission. I went to Izzie and executive producer Conrad Green with my idea. "I want to know what they go through," I told them. "I want to know what it feels like to train hard and put yourself out there dancing on live TV."

I had an intellectual understanding, to be sure. Anybody would. It's got to be frightening and exciting all at once. But knowing that in my head was very different from feeling it in every nerve ending of my body. And it was that significant difference that I hoped would improve my hosting of the show.

Conrad and Izzie said OK. That was the easy part. Now Ashly had to teach me the quickstep. That was the hard part (mostly for her).

It all seems obvious now. In those initial weeks that made up the first season, through the *Dance-off,* and into the beginning of season two, I was standing slightly apart from the proceedings. A bit like Bob Saget stood at arm's length from *America's Funniest Home Videos* when he was on camera. I used scripted jokes when I'd join the couples after their dance. I used scripted jokes when I sent the couples backstage to await the judges' verdict. Some of the jokes were really good, but none of them were organic to the live show going on all around me. By dancing on the show with Ashly, I was forcing myself to totally experience the "now" of it. It would shift my focus in the same way *Hollywood Squares* producer Steve Radosh helped me to do when he told me, "Your main job is to take care of the contestants."

Years earlier, a mime would make me a better broadcaster. Now a ballroom dancer would make me a better host. The shortest distance between two points isn't *always* a straight line.

For my network-television dancing debut, I thought the quickstep was a perfect choice. Ashly wasn't so sure.

"It's one of the most difficult ballroom dances," she told me. "Why did you pick this one?"

I had my reasons. The truth is, for me, any dance was going to be difficult. Just avoiding "white man's overbite" the moment I began moving to the music was going to be difficult. But the quickstep gave me comedic maneuvering room. And I was going to need it.

I wanted the dance to be an homage to Stan Laurel, Dick Van Dyke, Charlie Chaplin, Buster Keaton, and all the other physical comedians I'd loved since childhood. The producers gave us a list of songs from which we could choose. Judy Garland's version of "Get Happy" fit the bill perfectly.

Over a three-week period, Ashly and I squeezed in as many hours of training as I could. When it became clear she needed backup (one person can do only so much when training two left feet), she called in another of our professional dancers from season two, Nick Kosovich. Nick had been partnered with actress Tatum O'Neal, who was voted off after the second week. Nick had some time on his hands, and Ashly had her hands full. A perfect match.

Keeping proper form was one of my biggest problems. My upper right arm, which was supposed to stay parallel to the floor, kept heading south. My head was droopy, too. Nick's solution? A broomstick and a pencil. He placed the broomstick on the back of my neck and had me wrap my arms around it to achieve a perfect hold. Then, to keep my head from nodding forward, he placed an unsharpened pencil between my chin and my sternum. I looked like a student at the Marquis de Sade Dance Academy. But it helped.

One of the easiest things in the process was arriving at the story line of the dance. While Ashly was teaching me about dancing, I was giving her a crash course in silent-film comedians and their modern-day counterparts. But while I wanted to make the dance funny, I also wanted people to see that I took the discipline seriously. First and foremost, this had to have all the signature moves of a quickstep. Only then could I indulge myself.

"This should be a courtship story," I said, ignoring for the time being that I was older than Ashly's dad. "Your character is a flirt and mine is a klutz. The more I try to impress you, the clumsier I get." This gave me ample room for a few touches of Stan Laurel and a lot of Chaplin and Dick Van Dyke.

After I bobble my bowler cap in an attempt to dazzle her, Ashly's character takes me by the hand, and, as the song and dance progresses, my pratfalling paramour begins gaining in confidence. By the end of the dance I've literally swept her off her feet.

The three weeks we trained were nothing short of an emotional rollercoaster. I experienced everything from euphoria to frustration to abject horror. At one point, while I was experiencing the horror, Izzie offered me the out of prerecording the dance.

"We'll tape it that afternoon and role it into the live show," she said. "It'll be fine."

"I can't," I said instantly, not even considering the escape clause. "The whole reason I wanted to do this is to really know what they go through. If I don't do it live I'm playing it safe. They don't have that option. And I wouldn't have the whole experience."

That and the decision to do it in the first place were the two smartest choices I made.

The rehearsals with Ashly taught me more than just the quickstep. I learned more about the life of a competitive ballroom dancer in those three weeks than I'd gained from a season and a half of hosting the show. We talked about the level of commitment, the camaraderie, and the competition that were a constant part of all their lives. Most of our pros knew and competed against each other. They were both personal friends and professional rivals.

Our most recent season is the perfect example of that. Corky Ballas, the professional partner of Oscar- and Emmy-winning actress Cloris Leachman, is the father of season-six champion Mark Ballas and teacher to professional dancer Derek Hough and his sister, two-time *DWTS* champion (and my favorite country singer next to Sara Evans) Julianne Hough. In ballroom dancing as in Disneyland, it's a small world after all.

Not only was I learning about what the stars went through, which was my original goal in deciding to dance, but I was also learning more about their partners as well.

A few hours prior to the live broadcast of the results show on which Ashly and I were to perform, we had our dress rehearsal. Dress rehearsals on *Dancing with the Stars* are the R-rated version of the actual show. The reason for that is, well, me. I swear a lot during the dress rehearsals. And I tell suggestive jokes. And I attempt to break up the stars, the band, and the technical staff. ABC and the producers have warned people who attend the dress that "Tom may get a bit colorful." I do that partly to amuse myself, but mostly to relax the couples before the live performance.

On this particular day I was in need of a laugh or two myself. I was nervous. Ashly and I were about to perform the quickstep in front of the remaining season-two cast, and I realized, for the first time, that *this* was the audience I was performing for. I wasn't really doing this for the home viewer. I wasn't even doing it for me. I was doing it for them. It was my way of saying, "I get it. What you're doing takes (no anatomical disrespect intended) really large balls."

In the dress rehearsal, as in the broadcast performance, the off-camera voice of the British announcer proclaimed, "Dancing the quickstep, Tom Bergeron and his partner, Ashly DelGrosso." Then Harold Wheeler and the band struck up the opening notes of "Get Happy," and Beverley Staunton, one of our incredibly versatile singers, brought Judy Garland's sound back to life. It went great. At the end the cast and crew offered their congratulations. The hard part was over.

Now I just had to do it for twenty million people.

By the time we got to the live broadcast I was concerned that I was *too* relaxed. I'd been so relieved that the pros and stars enjoyed our performance that I was treating the actual show like a rehearsal. Unwittingly, our singer, Beverley, snapped me back to reality.

Each time Ashly and I danced, I ad-libbed a different move at the top to try to break her up. Sometimes it was a face, other times a gesture, but always the goal was to see her smile. One could argue I should have paid more attention to just keeping my feet untangled, but her smile was worth the risk. What I hadn't planned on was that I'd break up Beverley, too. And she'd forget to sing.

On the live broadcast everything started smoothly. The British announcer announced, Harold and the band played, and Ashly and I began to dance. But there was no Beverley. Judy Garland was off in the Oz-zone. Suddenly I was *extremely* aware of being on live television in front of twenty million people.

Where's the singing? Where's the singing? What do I do now? Did I miss my lockstep? Oh, shit. . . .

And then I heard her voice. She'd missed only a few seconds, but as people often say when they're about to slam their car into a bridge abutment, I had the sensation of time slow . . . ing . . . down. When Beverley began singing, balance was restored to the space-time continuum, and I was a much happier quickstepper.

And I hadn't missed the lockstep. It was exactly as Kelly Monaco described it to me after her wardrobe malfunction. Your mind is dealing with other things, but your body keeps dancing. While part of me was approaching panic mode, my slightly addled muscle memory took over.

"Well, you got the whole experience," Ashly told me later. She explained that in professional ballroom competition, dealing with the unexpected is just part of the job. Sometimes music cues are missed, couples on crowded dance floors career into each other like sequined bumper cars, and precise choreography turns clumsy. It's how you roll with the punches that matters in the end.

You can probably see our quickstep on YouTube, so I can't get away with pretending it deserved tens from the judges. Fives, maybe. Len Goodman, charmer that he is, said my dancing was worthy of *America's Funniest Home Videos*. Go take a look and judge for yourself. Ashly, for dealing with both Master P and me in a single season, deserved a *Spinal Tap* score: she deserved an eleven.

I like to think that I'd be a much better student now and that I could hold my form without poking a pencil in my sternum. I've certainly seen a lot more dancing since season two and have a better sense of what each style requires. But I'm in no hurry to dance again on the show. It's a lot of work. Hosting is much easier. Or at least it *became* a lot easier after I danced.

My quickstep with Ashly marked the turning point for me. Out went the scripted jokes following the couples' dances and almost everywhere else. My friend and longtime coworker Dave Boone, a very funny guy, had to endure script meetings where I "killed his babies" much as I had done to the writers on *AFV.*

Initially the producers were nervous. To them I was like the Jack Kevorkian of jokes. But eventually they saw that my goal wasn't to be serious; my goal was to be present.

In the place of the written material, I just reacted to what I saw live (or "LIIIIVE") and in the moment. If I was genuinely moved, I said so. If I felt like being a wiseass, I did so. But it was real. It was organic. And the adrenaline rush of being, as Tony would have said, "on the deck" made it feel like a different show.

By the time I began hosting *Dancing with the Stars* I'd been meditating for about thirty years. That's *three decades* of an almost daily practice of putting my ass in a chair and focusing my energy into the present moment. And it *still* took me a while to find my way.

So the next time you're kicking yourself for missing something obvious in your own life, relax. It happens. Even when it should be as clear as the mantra on your face.

34

DANCE PARTNERS

CHERYL BURKE, CARRIE ANN INABA, AND I WERE SITTING BACK-stage at the CNN studios on Sunset Boulevard in Los Angeles. We, along with several other *Dancing with the Stars* cast members getting primped and powdered in the makeup room, were going to appear as guests on *Larry King Live*. He was devoting his entire show to spotlighting ours.

"How long do you think this will last?" Cheryl asked me.

"This?" I said, missing her point. "An hour."

"Not *Larry King,* dummy. I mean *our* show."

It was a good question. And I had a good answer. "I don't know. It depends."

"On what?"

"On whether we can remember how it feels right now. What we've got here is lightning in a bottle. We're on a hit. It's new, it's exciting, and we're all fond of each other. But watch any *True Hollywood Story* and you can see how quickly it can all go south. Ratings matter, obviously, but sometimes shows die before the audience catches on. They die from the inside. People forget that they're part of a team, or they forget what it felt like before they were on a hit. As long as we don't lose sight of that, I can see this going for another four or five years."

"Really?" Cheryl said. "You think it could go that long?"

"Absolutely. As long as we keep enjoying ourselves, the viewers probably will, too."

Five years isn't really *that* long a time, but, as I wrote before, most TV shows have the life span of a hummingbird. Even surprise hits can burn out quickly (*Joe Millionaire,* anyone?), let alone survive half a decade. So many factors can work against you (bad scheduling; *overscheduling,* like with Regis's *Millionaire;* a new hot show opposite you on another network; etc.) that you'd best take care of the things you *can* control. And chief among them is the energy you bring to the set.

What I was telling Cheryl in essence was this: enjoying it *now* rather than looking back after it's over and wishing you had *then* is also good for job security. Hollywood is full of faded stars who were so busy keeping score that they forgot to have fun with the game. And once *they* weren't having fun, their audience left them for someone who was.

When I signed my original contract with Vin Di Bona for *America's Funniest Home Videos,* it was for six years. I had never signed a contract for that length of time, and I was hesitant. Ken Lindner, who represented me at the time (Babette had moved from his agency to ICM, and I hadn't yet joined her there), advised me not to worry.

"Vin's own lawyer told me the show won't last that long," Ken said. The lawyer wasn't being disloyal. He was merely stating a likely fact. Most shows don't.

I'm now in my ninth year with *AFV.* The show itself is approaching it's twentieth. When my six-year deal was up I signed for an additional five. I'm still having fun. After all, what's not to like about babies making poopy faces or grooms passing out during wedding vows? They've helped make *America's Funniest Home Videos* the longest-running prime-time entertainment show in ABC's history. So when it comes to scientifically predicting program longevity, clearly all bets are off. Slapstick has remarkable staying power. Somewhere the Three Stooges are smiling.

How long will *Dancing with the Stars* last? I don't know. I do know
that on that last show, whenever it is, I'll be able to say I enjoyed almost every minute of it. Even Master P's dancing. And that will have
had less to do with the great ratings than with the great people. On
DWTS, as with *Hollywood Squares, Videos,* and the rest, most of my
favorite moments have happened *off* the air.

Like the time I was straddled in public by Heather Mills.

GET BACKGET BACKGET BACK

It was midway through season four of *DWTS.* I was throwing a party
for the staff at Social, a club on Sunset Boulevard in Hollywood. The
party had been going for a few hours.

I was facedown on the carpet. And sober.

Several coworkers stood around the pool table watching as
Heather Mills positioned herself over my back. A close game of bil-
liards doubles had been under way, Heather and I pitted against
Dancing executive producer Conrad Green and another staffer, when
somehow the conversation turned to aching muscles. The moment I
mentioned my past history of back spasms, Heather made the offer.

"Let me crack your back."

"Excuse me?"

"Get down on your stomach and I'll crack your back."

I wasn't sure this was a good idea. "I don't know."

"Come on," she insisted. "I used to do this for Paul all the time."

"Great," I said, a bit too quickly. "And we all know how well *that*
turned out."

It probably wasn't the smartest thing to say to a high-profile di-
vorcée about to hammer her palms along your spine.

Still, I did as directed and got down on my stomach. Suddenly I
had the former Mrs. Paul McCartney perched on my butt. She leaned
forward with her hands resting just south of my neck. I had a strange
thought in that moment. *Would I have let Yoko Ono do this?*

With surprising strength and speed Heather went to it, applying pressure in synchronized fashion from my neck to my tailbone. As she'd promised, I felt a few cracks along the way. When she dismounted I slowly got to my feet. "Wow," I admitted, "that was incredible." It really was. I felt great.

"Anytime," she said.

Months later, during a rehearsal with the season-five cast, Heather's season-four dance partner, Jonathan Roberts (now paired with Marie Osmond), was talking to her on his cell phone. He called me over. "Heather wants to say hi," he said.

After a few pleasantries I told her, "I never walk past a pool table without thinking of you."

She was flattered. I think.

SEXY**SEXY CARROTS**SEXYCARROTS

On numerous occasions at *Dancing with the Stars* I've been offered a spray tan. I've resisted, even going so far as to profess on air that I prefer the "pasty, middle-aged-man look." It makes for a nice contrast with all the bronzed, buff dancers. Or so I keep telling myself. I may not appear quite as sun-dappled as the others, but at least I don't risk looking like a walking vegetable. Plus, I'd already been Mr. Tomato Head once in Las Vegas, and that was plenty.

Kym Johnson and Cheryl Burke, two of our pro dancers, were on the phone. They were calling to tell me they were running a little late.

"No problem," I said. "I'll see you when you get here." Would I ever.

After turning down several invitations to join them and the other pros at area nightspots after the show (I'd rather be in REM sleep than on TMZ at midnight), I'd invited them to a weekend dinner in my neck of the woods. We were going to meet at my house, then head to the restaurant. The moment they turned into the driveway and I caught sight of Kym's blonde hair, I could tell something wasn't quite right.

I peered into the car as they pulled to a stop. "You're orange," I said to Kym. "You look like a sexy carrot." Then I turned to Cheryl. She, too, was an odd shade, but under her brunette hair it wasn't as obvious at first. "What the hell happened?" I asked them.

They were both mortified. "They tried out a new spray tan on us," Kym said. "It's horrible."

Cheryl added, "We've been changing colors all the way here."

By the time we got to the restaurant the two of them had achieved a shade somewhere between pumpkin and Oompa-Loompa. We made sure to get a table outside in the shade. And way in the back.

APINCHA PINCH OF SPICEAPINCHOFSPICE

Live television not only provides *me* with opportunities; it provides our celebrities and pros with them as well. During season five, Spice Girl Mel B and her partner, Maksim Chmerkovskiy, decided I was looking much too relaxed on air. So, in the spirit of mucking about, they decided to try to trip me up. Their tactic? Blatant sexual harassment. And, at Mel's hand at least, I loved it.

It was the third week of competition. They had completed their jive and stood by me to hear the judges' comments. Afterward, just as I was throwing to a commercial, Mel began a slinky shimmy into my left side. It felt great, but, as she and Max had hoped, it caught me by surprise.

"I think I've lost my place," I said, deciding to abandon the scripted tease for the flesh-and-blood tease sliding up my suit.

"I think there's more show coming," I continued as Mel wiped some very real sweat off my brow. "Who cares, really?"

In subsequent weeks they upped the ante. Mel added butt pinches to the shimmy, but by then I was not only ready for it, I was looking forward to it. Lois understood, thankfully, although she was mercilessly teased by her girlfriends for allowing a Spice Girl to grope her husband.

On the finale, which pitted Mel B and Max against Helio Castroneves and Julianne Hough for the mirror-ball trophy, I exacted a
well-toned measure of revenge. As Mel stood at my side listening to
the judges' critiques of their final dance, I waited until I was off camera and grabbed myself a handful of Spice Girl buttock.

Turn-a-butt fair play.

THROW**THROW ME A BONE**THROWMEABONE

Following one of our Tuesday results shows during season six, I went
to LAX to take the red-eye to Chicago to tape *Oprah*. She was doing
a show the next morning spotlighting *America's Funniest Home Videos*. If the flight left as scheduled, I'd have time to land, get to the
hotel, shower, shave, steam my suit, and immediately hightail it to
Harpo Studios for the taping. With luck I'd grab a couple of hours'
sleep on the plane. As I made my way to the security checkpoint at
the United Airlines terminal, a typically jaunty TMZ duo appeared
out of nowhere. They're like tabloid ninjas.

"Hi, Tom, how're ya doin'?" Their tone is always disarmingly
friendly and as heartfelt as a pick-up line in a bar.

"Fine," I said, not quite sure why they'd zeroed in on me. I figured
it must have been a slow celebrity-sighting night. I'm a bit outside
their demo.

They quickly got to the point. "What do you think about [and
here they named two of our latest cast members rumored to be engaging in horizontal rehearsals]?"

Considering my evasive options, I settled for an air of mock in-
dignation. "I'll tell you what I think," I said. "I think that after five
and a half seasons no one ever links *me* with *anyone*! What am I?
Chopped liver? For god's sake throw me a bone, will you? Is it *that*
hard to believe?"

They both laughed. I guess it is.

FATHER**FATHER TOM**FATHERTOM

And I know why. On the Hollywood Cool Meter, I give off a vibe closer to Tom Bosley (*Happy Days, Father Dowling Mysteries*) than Tom Cruise (hyper dude, fathered Suri). While it's true I'm old enough to be the father of most of our pro dancers, and *can* be a bit of a dad around them (*"How much are you smoking?" "You're burning the candle at both ends a lot, aren't you?" "You've got to take care of yourself"*), when it comes to our stars, I'm more often father confessor.

On a number of occasions over seven seasons of *DWTS*, I've answered a knock on my dressing-room door and found one of our stars asking to talk to me.

"I don't think the producers like me," one said.

"I think there's a conspiracy," declared another.

No one ever stops by to celebrate their high scores or, at the other end of the spectrum, discuss their wobbly dancing. It's always about conspiracies.

"They told me to make sure I ask for viewer votes," one complained to me about the producers. "Why would they do that?"

I wondered if this person had ever actually *watched* the show.

"Because the viewer votes count for half of your scores," I reminded them in a tone I used often with my daughters. When they were in grade school. "Viewer votes are extremely important."

The star, who, not surprisingly, did not go on to win the mirrorball trophy, remained unconvinced. "I still think it's rigged."

HALLWAY**HALLWAY NEIGHBORS**HALLWAYNEIGHBORS

During our spring season of *Dancing with the Stars,* CBS Television City, where we shoot the show, is also home to *American Idol.* That's right, the biggest shows on ABC and Fox originate from studios owned by CBS. Years ago, when variety shows were all the rage, CBS had, at any given time, *The Carol Burnett Show*, *The Red Skelton Show*, *Sonny and Cher*, *The Smothers Brothers*, *Glen Campbell*, *Tony Orlando and Dawn*, et cetera occupying their soundstages and their network schedule. When that format went the way of the western, CBS Television City shifted, with the exception of some daytime soaps and *The Price Is Right*, to largely being the landlord for other networks' shows.

During the spring season the dressing room directly across the hall from mine belongs to *Idol* judge Paula Abdul. Paula, a major *DWTS* fan, often sneaks into our studio on Tuesdays when *American Idol* signs off for the night. She hangs out in the backstage area to cheer on the couples and watch the special dance numbers on the results show. On a few occasions she's even sat on camera at a ringside table. She's made no secret of her desire to actually be a contestant on the show, but my guess is that the higher-ups at Fox aren't too keen on the idea.

Paula's dressing room is always packed with people. It's impressive. I'm usually sitting alone in mine watching cable news. I'll admit it; I occasionally get jealous that she has "people." I don't know what I'd do with "people" if I had them hanging around my dressing room all day. I'd probably ask them to leave so I could get back to watching MSNBC. Still, every so often I wonder what it would be like.

Outside her door a rather imposing gentleman stands guard. One day I asked him for a favor.

"Could you occasionally stand over here by my door, too? And use the scary face if anyone approaches?"

"Sure," he said.

"Thanks. Usually the only time I have security around me is when they're giving me the wand at the airport."

Later that afternoon as I was returning from snacking at the craft-services table, he was standing by my door with crossed arms and a stern expression.

"That's great," I said as I approached. "Very impressive."

"And you are . . . ?" he asked. He was kidding, thankfully. No way I was getting in there if he wasn't.

During the fall of 2006 William Shatner was a hallway neighbor. This was a particular treat for me as I'd been a fan of his for years, through the original *Star Trek* TV series and movies, *T.J. Hooker,* and, of course, *Boston Legal.* I'd interviewed him several times during my *Breakfast Time* and *Fox After Breakfast* period and always enjoyed him as a guest, too.

Bill was hosting a short-lived ABC game show called *Show Me the Money!* The show, a variation on NBC's hit *Deal or No Deal* (and produced by the same company, Endemol USA), featured contestants answering trivia questions for big cash prizes. Instead of gorgeous models holding briefcases containing dollar amounts, *Show Me the Money* featured gorgeous dancers (including a pre–*Dancing with the Stars* Julianne Hough) holding *scrolls* containing dollar amounts. Apparently it's easier to dance holding a scroll than a briefcase.

Bill was, as always, a force of nature. I sat in the audience for about an hour just to watch him work and marveled at his energy. But unlike the live telecasts of *Dancing, Show Me the Money* was a taped show. And . . . it . . . took . . . forever. A crew member later told me that one of the shows took around four hours to shoot. I would have run screaming from the studio after three. The delays weren't due to Bill. Mostly they arose from the usual start-up speed bumps that taped shows have the unfortunate luxury to indulge. By the time the show wrapped for the night it should have been called *Show Me the Mattress.*

During one of his breaks, and knowing that he and his wife, Elizabeth, are *Dancing* fans, I suggested he come into the ballroom and watch the show in person.

"You can sit where I do while the couples are dancing," I told him. "It's off camera. You can come and go as you please."

"I can't," he said. "But I do have a favor."

I was intrigued. "Sure. Name it."

At that I swear Captain Kirk actually looked a bit shy. "I'd like to meet Edyta," he said. Bill was referring to Edyta Sliwinska, one of our professional dancers. I think he was speaking for almost every straight man or gay woman who'd ever watched the show.

When I did bring Edyta to meet him as he was in the hallway conferring with the *Show Me the Money* producers, I realized I really *had* seen a touch of shyness earlier. As Bill looked up after I called out, "I have someone here who wants to say hi," he caught sight of Edyta and said, "Oh, please, don't do this to me." It was quite charming, actually. The famous intergalactic Lothario was blushing like a schoolboy.

BACKBACK IN THE GAME?BACKINTHEGAME?

After one of the results shows during season seven, I was leaving the Television City lot to rendezvous with some friends for an after-show drink. I waited at a security gate as several people came back onto the lot through the revolving steel bars. One of them was Drew Carey. He's not a hallway neighbor, but he does shoot *The Price Is Right* on the same stage where I'd shot *Hollywood Squares*.

"Hey, Drew," I said as I extended a hand. "Tom Bergeron. Good to see you."

"We've missed you at the game-show-hosts meetings," he teased after we'd chatted a bit.

"I know," I said, hanging my head. "And I feel terrible about it."

If such meetings existed, I'm not sure if I could still claim membership. I haven't hosted a game show since *Hollywood Squares* ended production in 2004. But I came close to renewing that membership in 2007 when I was asked to consider hosting another game show. Although, to be honest, it wasn't *just* another game show I was being pitched.

It was *The Price Is Right*.

35

SOMETHING TO PLINKO-VER

MAY 22, 2007, WAS THE DATE OF THE SEASON-FOUR FINALE OF *Dancing with the Stars.* But more significantly for me and Lois, it was also our twenty-fifth wedding anniversary.

With our daughters' blessings and with a friend helping to mind the store in Connecticut, Lois had flown out from New York for the occasion. Early on the morning of May 23, after shaking off the remnants of the previous evening's wrap party, we drove up the Pacific Coast Highway to spend a few romantic days at a spa in Ojai.

As we were checking in, my cell vibrated. It was Babette.

"Fremantle wants to talk with you," she said. Fremantle is the production company behind *American Idol,* among other shows.

"What about?"

"*The Price Is Right,*" she said. *That's* one of the other shows.

I was surprised. "But I took myself out of the running for that months ago."

"I know," she said. "They still want to talk about it."

As any devotee of American pop culture knows, 2007 marked the end of Bob Barker's incredible thirty-five-year run as host of *The Price Is Right.* I had heard flattering rumors that my name was on the producers' short list for possible replacements, but, as the host of two prime-time ABC shows, I couldn't see how I could also, either contractually or physically, add the iconic CBS daytime show to my (no pun intended) dance card.

It turned out that contractually, anyway, I could.

"You're only exclusive to ABC in prime time," Babette reminded me. "You're free to do syndication or daytime."

She was right. I'd filled in numerous times on CBS's *The Early Show* both during Bryant Gumbel's tenure and in the weeks following his departure. At the time, I was also doing *Hollywood Squares* in syndication and *America's Funniest Home Videos* for ABC. As with my late-'90s stint on *Good Morning America,* there had been some press speculation that I'd take *The Early Show* job full-time. Unlike the *GMA* experience, it was never anything more than that. I liked being "the fill-in guy." The prospect of a regular 3:30 a.m. alarm, regardless of the show, had zero appeal.

For me, *The Price Is Right* also felt wrong. A large part of it was that I didn't want to spend any more time away from Lois and the girls by doing another show in Los Angeles. But also, contractual loopholes or not, I felt at home with ABC. It was a good fit. I didn't want to jeopardize that relationship by suddenly "seeing other people."

At the time, Babette smiled politely and didn't pursue it. But now, months later, the *Price* producers wanted to talk to me and she wanted me to listen to them. "I respect what you're saying about your relationship with ABC," she said. "I know you and Anne Sweeney go back to your days at fX. But your first loyalty is to Lois and the girls. This show could make you set for life."

Unwilling to abbreviate our anniversary interlude, and with reservations to fly back east directly afterward, I promised, if only out of professional courtesy, to talk with them by phone when Lois and I returned to Connecticut.

About a week later a conference call was arranged. As the Fremantle executives began making their pitch, I felt like I was attending my own funeral.

In a good way. It was like being eulogized without the awkward necessity of dying first.

They were flattering in the extreme, particularly when they told me that Bob Barker not only was aware of their call but supported it. That meant a lot to me. My ego was definitely getting a fluffing.

They explained that their production schedule called for 175 *Price Is Right* shows per season. They said they could work around my schedules for *Dancing with the Stars* and *America's Funniest Home Videos*. And then, echoing Babette's main selling point, they suggested that *The Price Is Right* could be my home for years.

I promised I'd mull it over, but as we hung up I already knew my answer. And it was all about home.

The only thing that made the long separations from Lois and the girls tolerable was the knowledge that we'd have large chunks of time together between *Dancing* seasons. If I added *Price* I'd be in California then as well. Captain Spasm could well make a comeback. And it would also beg the question *If I'm working so much that I never see my family, what exactly is the point of all this?*

The next morning I sent off an e-mail expressing my deep appreciation for their overture and my profound respect for Bob Barker and his remarkable career achievement. I reminisced about the times he and I had already crossed paths. In 2004 we'd shared a Daytime Emmy. For the six years of weekend tapings for *Hollywood Squares,* which we taped on the same stage as *The Price Is Right,* I used Bob's dressing room. Plus, years earlier, when we'd first met on *Breakfast Time,* not only had we played "Hard Hat Price Is Right" with the guys fixing a burst water main on Fifth Avenue, but he'd also shown me how to take a punch as he had from Adam Sandler in *Happy Gilmore.* Other than with Bob Barker, I'd never shared a room or a major award with someone who took a swing at me. We had a history.

I wrote that whoever took over *The Price Is Right* had big, iconic shoes to fill. And then I told them that, flattered as I was by their interest, I needed to keep some balance (and a wife and two daughters) in my life. And so I respectfully passed.

The next day Babette, to whom I'd forwarded a copy of the e-mail, was on the line. "Now they *really* want to talk."

I was stunned. "But I said no again."

"I know," she agreed. "But you said no so charmingly they wanted to offer a possibility."

"A possibility?"

"What if they moved the show to New York?"

Now I was *really* stunned. "They would do that?"

"They're willing to consider it if it would change your mind."

My mind raced. *Would* that make it feasible? I did miss working in Manhattan. But what would that mean for the production crew in California? They'd lose their means of support for *their* families so I could spend more time with mine? The karmic payback on that could be a bitch.

I needed to talk to Lois.

"Let us think about this," I told Babette.

"Fine," she said. "But think about the big picture."

When I told Lois about the latest curveball, she was as astounded as I had been. "That's amazing," she said.

"I know. I'm a little blindsided. They've really reached out with this. I feel strange just saying no again like a broken record."

"True," she said. "But would moving the show to New York really make it easier?"

I considered that for a moment. "Probably not. I'd end up flying even more than I do now."

"What if you sign for only a year?" Lois said. "See how it feels. I'll be in California a lot more once both girls are in college. That's right around the corner. We'd be fine."

Being married to a former television producer definitely had its advantages. Lois, like Babette, knew how to take the long view.

"Even if they don't go for it," I said, "at least it's worth a try."

Suddenly energized to the idea, I decided to spring into action. I was going to offer Fremantle a completely mapped out counter-proposal. But first I needed three things: a calendar, a crab-cake sandwich, and a martini.

I grabbed a notebook calendar from Lois's office and drove to my favorite local restaurant for the crucial remaining items. Sitting at the bar as the afternoon lunch crowd thinned, I began mapping out the next fourteen months. Starting with the two set seasons for *Dancing with the Stars* and likely shoot schedule for *America's Funniest Home Videos*, I deconstructed *The Price Is Right*'s production season and rebuilt it into a schedule that would still afford me chunks of time back east. *And* keep the show in Los Angeles.

It was a Hail Mary pass to be sure, but it felt much better than just saying no. I showed the finished product to Lois, and she agreed it looked doable. I passed it on to Babette, who in turn sent it along to the *Price* gang.

Silence.

No response. The flurry of communication came to a stop. As we waited for some feedback on my one-year counterproposal, the entertainment press was abuzz with Rosie O'Donnell's trip to Los Angeles to discuss becoming the new *Price Is Right* host. Rosie had made no secret of her desire to succeed Bob. The producer part of my brain could see the upside of that scenario. Rosie loved the show, and millions love Rosie. Given her charismatic and controversial personality, there'd be no shortage of press surrounding her initial shows. I presumed the sounds of silence wouldn't be broken until after she'd met with Fremantle and CBS head Les Moonves.

I was right. But, as it turned out, it wasn't due solely to Rosie's meeting. The proposal I'd offered, which was seriously considered, presented too many speed bumps for CBS and Fremantle in the end. Because of my ABC contract, I'd never be able to host a prime-time CBS *Price Is Right* special. Plus, *Price* would contractually have to be in third position behind *America's Funniest Home Videos* and *Dancing with the Stars*. That's the equivalent of telling someone that you want to have a relationship with them as long as your other spouses get first dibs.

Last, but not least, was my requirement for a one-year mutual trial period. CBS understandably wanted to announce the *new* host of *Price,* not the *new but we might be looking again in twelve months* host. And with the personable Drew Carey in the role, I think they did just fine.

But Bob Barker and I weren't done crossing paths. In late 2007 in Los Angeles, at an event celebrating the seventieth birthday of AFTRA (the American Federation of Television and Radio Artists), I was honored to present Bob with a Lifetime Achievement Award. And maybe one of these days, since he has more time on his hands, he might want to "come on down" to our little ballroom and show that kid Cloris Leachman what an older guy can do. You know, if the price is right.

Now that I definitely wasn't adding *Price* to my schedule, I had some extra time as well. Time enough to shoot thirteen episodes of an eco-oriented talk show/dinner party called *Supper Club* for Discovery's new Planet Green network in the spring of 2008. And time enough to cohost the 60th Primetime Emmy® Awards for ABC that fall.

On *Supper Club* we talked a lot about how to save the planet.

On the Emmys I became more concerned about how to save *myself.*

36

YIN, YANG, AND
YOUR MAMA

URING ONE OF OUR SEASON-SEVEN RESULTS SHOWS ON *DANC-ing with the Stars* we showcased all of the injuries that plagued our cast up to that point. Olympian Misty May-Treanor ruptured her Achilles tendon, comedian Jeffrey Ross suffered a scratched cornea, Derek Hough briefly knocked himself out after tripping over a light fixture, while Edyta Sliwinska, Brook Burke, and Susan Lucci all suffered twisted ankles and other foot infirmities. A few weeks after that segment aired, two-time *DWTS* champion (and Derek's sister) Julianne Hough had surgery to have her appendix removed and treat a case of endometriosis. Two days later our newest pro, Lacey Schwimmer, also received a diagnosis of endometriosis. It was amazing. Hugh Laurie doesn't have as many medical emergencies on *House*.

After the segment, I ad-libbed, "This is why I host. You rarely hear of hosting injuries. Unless you count the Emmys."

I got a big laugh. It was the first big Emmy-related laugh I did get. At the Emmys I mostly got crickets.

If you weren't watching that night (and based on the ratings, you weren't alone), let me pick that psychological scab just a bit to share the story with you. I'm not doing it because I'm a masochist. I'm doing it because in the span of twenty-four hours, in full view of millions,

I received another valuable lesson in the wonders of yin and yang. Or, in other words, I was reminded that sometimes when "shit happens," you can use it as fertilizer.

REUTERS NEWS WIRE:
WEDNESDAY, SEPTEMBER 24, 2008

LOS ANGELES (Reuters)—Twenty-four hours after co-hosting one of the biggest ratings flops in Emmy history, ABC's "Dancing with the Stars" emcee Tom Bergeron presided over the top broadcast on opening night of U.S. television's new season.

Monday's two-hour season premiere of "Dancing with the Stars" averaged 21.3 million viewers to rank as the night's most watched show and lead ABC to a first-place finish in the overall network rankings, Nielsen Media Research reported on Tuesday.

It was certainly a more robust beginning than was presaged by Sunday's ABC broadcast of the 60th annual Primetime Emmys, which tied the record for the least watched presentation of the awards with an average audience of just 12.3 million viewers.

The awards telecast also drew some of the most scathing reviews in Emmy history, especially for the collective hosting duties shared by Bergeron and four fellow reality show emcees—Howie Mandell, Ryan Seacrest, Jeff Probst and Heidi Klum.

"The show never fully recovered after an opening clunker thanks to the five reality show hosts," read the caption in a review in the Los Angeles Times.

SEVER**SEVERAL WEEKS EARLIER . . .** SEVERALWEEKSEARLI

I was sitting in a coffee shop back home in Connecticut reading the *New York Times.* My daughter was getting her hair done nearby, and Dad was providing cab service. It was a beautiful summer afternoon. Days earlier I had been nominated in a new Primetime Emmy category for Best Reality Host. Life was good.

And then my cell phone vibrated.

Vicky Dummer, one of ABC's senior vice presidents, who oversees reality shows, was on the line. "The producers of the Emmys are thinking of having the five Best Reality Host nominees *host the Emmys,*" she said. "What do you think?"

"I think it's a lousy idea," I said. "First of all, I just want to go to the Emmys with Lois and sit in the audience. I want to enjoy myself. I don't want to *work.* And second, even though the other nominees are friends, we have different styles. It'll be a nightmare. It'll be like herding cats."

Actually that's what I was *thinking. This* is what I said:

"If the others are up for it, sure, I'll do it."

Oops.

Maybe I should have gone with my gut.

The 60th Primetime Emmys were broadcast on ABC Sunday, September 21, 2008. The five nominees for Best Reality Host—me (*Dancing with the Stars*), Heidi Klum (*Project Runway*), Howie Mandel (*Deal or No Deal*), Jeff Probst (*Survivor*), and Ryan Seacrest (*American Idol*)—hosted the show. Here are a few of the reviews.

Rick Bentley of McClatchy Newspapers: "Sunday night's telecast of the 60th Annual Emmy Awards set a new standard for awards shows. You could take every elephant Ringling Bros. and Barnum &

Bailey circus owns, feed them rancid chili and spoiled boiled eggs for a month, and they could not create a bigger stinker."

USA Today: "It was hideously awful from start to harried finish, dragged down by five amateurish reality anchors who would have been unwelcome as guests, let alone hosts."

And Mary McNamara of the *Los Angeles Times* said, "If we come away with nothing else from this year's Emmys, let us all agree that having a host with some experience actually entertaining people is not a luxury, it's a necessity. The show never quite recovered from its unforgivably bad opener or its less-than-useless hosts."

You may be wondering if it was really *that* bad. I mean, come on, "rancid chili"?? But trust me, those were some of the *good* reviews.

In the weeks between the announcement of the five of us as hosts and the fateful broadcast, several scripts and approaches for opening the show were written and rejected. Among them were several proposed pretaped sketches. One had each of us being "judged" worthy of hosting the show by Simon Cowell of *Idol* and Carrie Ann Inaba of *Dancing.* Another had each of us separately dissing the other nominees in a *Big Brother*–style confessional.

Heidi Klum suggested the idea of all of us walking onstage in identical tuxes. Hers would be a breakaway tux that, when broken away, would reveal the comely Klum of runway fame. Howie Mandel suggested we play off the fact that as reality hosts, we don't sing, dance, or tell jokes. (That part I think we got across pretty well.) Howie wanted to make the open looser, more improvisational. Jeff Probst was the voice of caution, worried that we'd go out there and bomb. (I think we did *that* pretty well, too.) Ryan Seacrest, having been out there hosting the previous year on his own, was just happy to share the bull's-eye. My only contribution was a variation on the pretape judging bit. I thought we should replace Simon and Carrie Ann with people like Hugh Laurie and Terri Hatcher. *They* should be the ones deciding if we were up to the task. After all, *we* were the newcomers to *their* party. If anyone would be naturally skeptical of this hosting decision, it would be television's established elite.

No one idea appealed to all of us. As show day approached, a patch-work quilt of several ideas was sewn together. On *the morning of the broadcast* the five of us joined Emmy producer Ken Ehrlich in my dressing room. We still hadn't agreed on an open.

Ken had been up half the night pounding out a couple of possibilities. One, which with the benefit of hindsight seems brilliant, had us simply walking out, saying how happy we were to be there, and introducing the first presenters. Five hosts. No waiting. The other, which I'd read as an e-mail attachment at six in the morning, was a tightened version of the opening that eventually aired. Ken had taken the best lines from Howie's, Jeff's, and Ryan's improvising the day before and put them into script form. As written, the entire open, including a game William Shatner helping me tear away Heidi's tux, would have run under two minutes. Here's a look at some of that script.

Oprah Winfrey introduces hosts after her opening comments.

(The five hosts come out onstage. All are in tuxedos.)

RYAN SEACREST: *This is awkward, that's exactly what we were going to say.*

JEFF: *But I think we could add this—that the five of us could not be more honored and proud to be here tonight as nominees with all of you.*

HOWIE: *I just want to say something too. Oprah's right, this medium informs and educates. You know my biggest fear? That the audience is going to be informed that having five reality hosts . . . maybe not the best idea!*

JEFF PROBST: *This is the biggest night in television, and for weeks we've been trying to figure out what it is we can do for an opening.*

HOWIE: *This is what we came up with . . .*

RYAN: *Turn around and look at the teleprompter. There's nothing on it!!*

HOWIE: *I mean this is reality, people . . . We are like the "Bridge to Nowhere!"*

JEFF: *Seacrest, what are we supposed to do?*

RYAN: *Well first, you've got to welcome people.*

JEFF: *Oprah did that . . .*

HOWIE: *What else do we need to do?*

RYAN: *Tell people about the 60th Anniversary.*

JEFF: *Oprah did it.*

HOWIE: *What's left for us?*

RYAN: *Nothing.*

JEFF: *Absolutely nothing.*

RYAN: *Tom, it's your network, you handle it.*

(Ryan, Jeff, and Howie exit stage right.)

Primetime Emmy® script material ©Academy of
Television Arts & Sciences.

From there Heidi and I briefly dissed the departed, William Shatner was invited to the stage, pop went Heidi's tux, and we left.

Granted, it wasn't Shakespeare. It might not even be vintage Carrot Top. But it had the advantage of brevity.

In the end, the guys preferred to improvise their section rather than have it on prompter. In fact, one of their requests was to take a shot of the blank teleprompter as proof that they had nothing. The shot was never taken, and the improv, fueled by performance adrenaline and nervous energy, expanded to almost three times its intended length. Unless you're Seinfeld, that's *way* too much time for a show to be about nothing.

As Heidi and I stood in silence waiting for the guys to wrap it up, I was mulling over several possibilities.

I'm hearing laughs. Maybe this is actually working.

If I scope out the theater's exits now, I can make a quicker escape.

It could be time to return to flexible tubing.

Actor Jeremy Piven, from HBO's *Entourage,* received the first Emmy following the opening bit. After his own opening joke bombed, he ducked for cover behind us.

"I could stand up here and just keep talking forever," he said. "Oh, right. That was the open."

It got a big laugh. I knew that there was no point rationalizing. We were screwed.

With five hosts splitting the remaining duties, there were long breaks between our appearances. Backstage, while the others continued to speculate that the evening was salvageable, I sat in a director's chair and meditated. At one point when I opened my eyes, Ryan, who'd been watching me, said, "You're pretty quiet."

I nodded. "I know. I was meditating. I want to be as centered as possible before I go back out there."

"I've got to learn to do that," he said.

"It helps," I told him. "Especially on a night like this."

For me, that night, giving myself a Zen tune-up backstage was crucial. Once you lose an audience, it's extremely difficult to get them back. In a format like the Emmys, it was impossible. The best I could hope for was to find my center, confidently take the stage, and salvage a bit of my dignity.

Until it was time to drop Heidi Klum on her ass.

Her hip, actually. The picture of her hoisting her dress to display a softball-sized bruise (alongside a smiling me doing a Vanna White impression) spanned the globe within hours.

I'd never met Heidi prior to the Emmy gig, but, as I told her in an e-mail the day after the ceremony, getting to know her was my favorite part of the otherwise bizarre experience. And not because of her supermodel status. She's got a dry, take-you-off-at-the-knees sense of humor that I loved. The bit that yielded the picture—a "This is drama" swoon into my arms followed by a "This is comedy" pratfall on the stage as I dropped her—was her idea. Had the open of the show not died, that bit, and Heidi's impressive kerplunk, arguably would have played much better. By that point, however, we were like pitchers who were three balls behind the count.

Heidi insisted on doing the pratfall without any hip padding. She'd already been bruised in rehearsal but was resolute. I had images of her husband, Seal, showing up on my doorstep to "have a little chat" about my manhandling his wife, and I worried that the drop, no matter how gingerly I meant for it to be, might mean a kiss from a rose on *my* grave, but I couldn't talk her out of it. On the plus side, I got to rehearse numerous Heidi swoons into my arms.

Jimmy Kimmel presented the first-ever Emmy for Best Reality Host in a sketch that came toward the end of the three-hour broadcast. The idea of the sketch was to put us through the same type of sadistic, drawn-out elimination process that contestants on our respective shows endure. Jimmy punctuated his sketch by acknowledging our hosting effort, saying to the audience, "Weren't they sufficient?" Hilarious.

Jeff Probst won the inaugural award for his skillful handling of the warring tribes on *Survivor.* I was happy for him. And I was happy for me, too. We'd agreed that whoever won the Emmy would close the show. This meant I didn't have to go back out there. I was done meditating for the night, anyway. My new plan was to focus solely on vodka martinis. I had my microphone off and my tie loosened before the next award was announced.

After the show, Lois, Babette, my lawyer Mike Adler, and his wife, Brenda, all strolled over to the Los Angeles Convention Center for the Governor's Ball. Along the way, several people offered cheery compliments on my work that evening. I smiled politely but took their kind words with a grain of salt. I was, after all, surrounded by actors.

I was braced for the reviews on Monday morning. I knew they were going to be scathing. But I also knew I had to shake them off and get to work. Monday evening I'd be back on the air, live, hosting the season-seven debut of *Dancing with the Stars*. Sure, twelve million people saw my belly flop on Sunday. I still needed to bring my A game for the twenty-one million who'd be watching on Monday.

Early Monday morning Lois and I were walking into the local Starbucks before I headed off to the studio. A friend sitting at an outside table called us over. He was reading the *Los Angeles Times*. "Nice picture," he said as he showed us the "Calendar" section. It wasn't bad. There I was, in full color, holding a swooning Heidi Klum. But then there was the headline.

A HOST OF PROBLEMS

I said to Lois, "I've got a line ready for tonight. If a couple gets a really bad score I'll tell them, 'At least you didn't have to host the Emmys.'"

"Don't do it," she said.

"Why not?"

"Don't make it about you. It's their first night dancing. They're all nervous. Your job is to make it about *them*."

She was right. And so that night, on the air, I never mentioned it. Off air, during our dress rehearsal, I did make a few jokes about it. Coming back from a faux commercial break, after tepid applause from the small assemblage of staff members and visitors in the seats, I said, "I got a better response at the Emmys."

My buddy Dave Boone was sitting nearby. "No, you didn't," he said.

Some friend! He'd completely ignored the adage that comedy equals tragedy plus time. It had been less than a *day*, for Chrissake!

But it was still pretty funny.

As the day progressed, several people commented that they'd seen some positive mentions, including one in a sidebar story in the *Los Angeles Times*. Denise Martin (who is now on my Christmas-card list) gave me five stars for being "always game and appropriately wry." NPR reported that *"Dancing with the Stars* host Tom Bergeron, an underrated performer with a long history of hosting game shows and talk shows . . . , managed to seem relaxed and funny and would have been a perfectly lovely solo host."

I'll be sending in my membership pledge tomorrow.

People magazine's online site reported a gratifying show of empathy among the stars in attendance. A surprised Michael Aussielo noted:

> *how hard it was to find a celeb in attendance that was willing to join Jeremy Piven in dumping on Howie, Heidi, Ryan, Tom, and Jeff—and I talked to a lot of celebs that night. "I'm just happy to be invited to the party," insisted Amy Poehler. "I'm cool with the entertainment." The funny lady's SNL boss, Lorne Michaels, who was in charge of the 40th Emmy telecast 20 years ago, went a step further, giving show producer Ken Ehrlich props for thinking outside the box. "They're still taking chances," he praised. Focusing on the positive—the one positive—30 Rock's Tina Fey declared, "I'm a big fan of Tom Bergeron."*

Given my massive Tina Fey crush (which Lois understands and many people share), seeing that quote was even better than winning the Emmy. Well, OK, pretty damn close anyway.

Walking onstage, regardless of the venue, is like strolling onto a high wire strung over a tattered net. When you're in the zone the high is exhilarating, but if you lose your balance the drop can be a bitch. What Michael Aussielo *did* find among the stars was possibly an appreciation for the attempt if not the result. Show me a performer who has never bombed, and I'll show you a performer who needs to get out more. It's inevitable. You'd just rather do it somewhere other than network television. But wherever it happens, the true test is whether you can, like the old Timex watch ads said, "take a lickin' and keep on tickin'."

And that's not just true for performers. Everyone, everywhere, steps onto his or her own version of that high wire every day. Hosts, actors, flexible-tubing salesmen, single parents, office clerks, police officers, politicians, doctors, lawyers, students, newlyweds, soldiers, and all the rest get out of bed every morning and step right up. It's called life.

"All the world's a stage," right? "And all [of us] merely players"? And that *is* Shakespeare.

You've reached the Zen School of Comedy. No one is here to take your call. At the tone, leave a message and your mama will get back to you.

BEEP. Hi, I'm suffering from PASS.

Pratfall Aversion Stress Syndrome?

Uh, yeah, that's it. Hey, wait a minute. I thought this was a recording.

Maybe it is.

But we're having a conversation.

Are we?

Look, I've got a real problem. This isn't a laughing matter.

Which is why you called the Zen School of Comedy?

I called to learn how to stop worrying about failing.

Accept that you will.

But I don't want to.

Tough.

Excuse me?

We have a saying in Zen Buddhism. "Everybody dies."

This is the comedy school?

It's whatever you want it to be.

And how does *that* work, exactly?

Humor requires perspective. Perspective requires focus. Focus requires balance. Balance requires attention to the present moment. In the "now" one is freed from labels. Success and failure, good luck and bad—they're all constructs of your mind.

And that's it? That's all I need to be free of PASS?

Yes. That and a rubber chicken.

I'd wager that in your own life there are events that, at the time, you thought to be major setbacks. Only later was it obvious those "setbacks" were really springboards for you to reach new heights. Cohosting the Emmys and, a day later, hosting the season premiere of *Dancing with the Stars* provided me with palpable proof of the yin and yang of things. On Sunday there were bad ratings and bad reviews. On Monday there were good ratings and good reviews.

Which was good luck and which was bad? It depends on your perspective.

I got a better chapter out of Sunday, but Monday gave me a chance to prove (mostly to myself) that all my talk about the value of "staying present" and "being in the moment" wasn't a pile of platitudes. It's true and it works.

Even after you've been compared to rancid chili.

37

BUT ENOUGH ABOUT ME

IT WAS FIVE THIRTY IN THE MORNING. THE OVERNIGHT STORM HAD dumped more snow than expected. On top of that, I'd overslept. I was in a mad rush to get to the radio station, but my frantic shoveling wasn't yielding results. My car was stuck. Several times after thinking I'd made headway, I revved the engine only to have the rear wheels spin right back into the snowdrift. The clock was ticking. My blood pressure was rising.

I lost it.

I began kicking the car, slamming the shovel into the snowdrift, and cursing a blue streak. No one else was outside the apartment complex at that hour to see me go ballistic. But, as I found out several days later, someone was watching me from his window.

"I saw you the other morning," a neighbor told me. "I was going to come out and help you, but I didn't dare to."

"I'm embarrassed," I said. "I was late, frustrated. I'm not excusing it, I just . . ."

"I understand," he said, gently cutting me off. "But I thought you should know."

I got the message. He wasn't just telling me he'd witnessed my display of snowdrift rage. He was subtly suggesting I look at the big picture causing my short fuse.

In the years following that humiliating morning, meditation became my primary looking glass. In all honesty, despite over thirty years of practice, I can't tell you that it provided the answer to *why* I'd been such a hothead. But it has kept me from continuing to be one.

"Really? You had a bad temper? I never would have guessed" has been the most gratifying response from friends when I've told them I'd be including that confession in this book.

None of them would dispute the fact that I can occasionally be stubborn as hell, or curmudgeonly, or, as my daughters could tell you, a bit of a fusspot. But an out-of-control, shovel-swinging hothead? Those days are long gone.

I largely credit my mantra. Some people prefer clown noses.

Actress Linda Gray, *Dallas*'s long-suffering Sue Ellen Ewing and my cohost for a week on *Fox After Breakfast,* is a proponent of the latter. Particularly in Los Angeles traffic when faced with *other* clowns on the verge of road rage.

"Rather than give in to that energy," she told me, "I reach over, put on the clown nose, and smile at them. They either laugh or decide I might be too crazy to mess with."

Linda and I met during my own "long-suffering" period as I wrestled with management over the direction of the Fox show. We'd had a number of conversations about my growing frustration. The week after she left I received a small package from her in the mail.

It was a box full of clown noses.

To this day it's still one of my all-time favorite gifts, a box full of bright, red, squeezable foam perspective.

If my temper was once my albatross, my sense of humor has often been my salvation. And it's proven to be one of the strongest branches on the family tree. In fact, one of my proudest moments as a father was when my daughters proved they could comically cut me down to size.

Lois was out for an evening with her girlfriends, and our daughters, then only four and two, were up a little past their bedtimes. This was during my WBZ Boston years, when I hosted the morning-drive radio show and then switched gears for a midday TV show. As I was facing a 4 a.m. alarm, their bedtime was pretty much my bedtime, too.

Despite my best efforts, the girls were stalling. We had been having fun together. They wanted to have more. I did, too, but I needed to get to bed. Four in the morning came much too quickly, and climbing out of bed at that hour never got easier.

"Girls, I mean it. Let's move," I grumped as they meandered toward the stairs.

I was right behind them as they slowly made their way up. Then, unable to contain myself, I burped out one more unnecessary "Daddy has to get up really early, you know."

At that Jessica turned and smiled. Over the previous week we'd been watching the film version of *Annie,* starring Carol Burnett and Albert Finney, on an almost continuous loop. Most parents of young children know what it's like to get caught in that *Groundhog Day* pattern of repeating the same favorite DVD over and over and over again. After about twenty viewings Lois and I were praying that the sun *wouldn't* come up yet again tomorrow.

In any case, Jessica heard something in the nagging tone of my voice that begged a response. And, at four years old, she gave me her biggest Annie smile and said, "We love you, Miss Hannigan."

I burst out laughing. It was the *perfect* line, delivered perfectly, and it took the piss right out of me. I was so proud of her comic timing my fusspot was emptied. As the girls have grown I've repeatedly been reminded of how risky it is for me to get on my high horse anywhere in their vicinity. When it comes to their dad, they have an unerring bullshit detector. I think they got it from Lois. I can't get anything past her, either.

And lest you think I'm trying to get anything past *you,* I just realized that after all of these stories you might still be waiting for me to address this book's subtitle. Let's do that now.

What's "the art of staying sane in Hollywood?" To me it's no different than the art of staying sane anywhere. Here are the key things I've learned:

Be. Here. NOW.
Don't forget to breathe.
When all else fails, grab a clown nose.

That's pretty much it. I firmly believe that adherence to those three things will keep you sane whether you're in Hollywood, Scranton, or a really slow line at the supermarket.

Oh, wait. There *are* a couple more things:

Never fall asleep in a tanning machine.
Try not to pee in the tub.

There. We're done.

I now return you to your regularly scheduled life.

ACKNOWLEDGMENTS

TO BABETTE PERRY FOR BEING SUCH A PEST, MIKE ADLER FOR LAYING down the law, Lisa Sharkey for risking her reputation, Adam Korn for his astute observations, Gene Boles, Cathy Levitan, Helen Tierney, and John D'Amelio for jogging my memory, Carl Reiner for putting the wind at my sails, Izzie Pick for her encouragement, and Lauren Graham for that punch line on the plane.

But I want to especially thank the late Edwin Johnson for opening the first door to my career.

And my rhyming parents, Kay and Ray, for assuring me that their door was always open.